THE VIBRANT RELATIONSHIP

Other titles in the
Systemic Thinking and Practice Series:
edited by Ros Draper
published and distributed by Karnac

Credit card orders, Tel: +44(0) 20-7431-1075; Fax: +44(0) 20 7435 9076
Email: shop@karnacbooks.com
www.karnacbooks.com

Kirsten Seidenfaden
Piet Draiby
Mette-Marie Davidsen and Ros Draper (Editors)

THE VIBRANT
RELATIONSHIP

A HANDBOOK FOR COUPLES AND THERAPISTS

First English edition published in 2011 by
Karnac Ltd
118 Finchley Road, London NW3 5HT

Copyright © 2011 to Kirsten Seidenfaden and Piet Draiby

First published in Danish as *Det levende parforhold* by
TV 2 Forlag © 2007

Second edition by
Lindhardt & Ringhof © 2009

British Library Cataloguing in Publication Data
A C.I.P. for this book is available from the British Library
       ISBN: 978-1-85575-813-1

The book was written in close co-operation with journalist and writer
Mette-Marie Davidsen.
The English version is edited in close co-operation with Ros Draper.

All illustrations in the book are by the artist Viktor IV.
They have been reproduced in agreement with Ina Elisabeth Munck.

Portrait of the authors: Miklos Szabo
Cover and graphics: Bramsen and Nørgaard
Translation by James Bulman-May

Edited and produced by The Studio Publishing Services Ltd
www.publishingservicesuk.co.uk
email: studio@publishingservicesuk.co.uk

Printed in Great Britain

DRINK WATER

70

DRINK
WATER

Betaald p.Kas 2 2 JAN. 1970

Now

← Red

the SPANISH WATER BOTTLE
Burlap wrapped—
painted WHITE

Madrid spring 1861

AMSTERDAM TIME

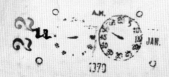

A.M.
JAN.
1970

TABLE OF CONTENTS

PART 1

PART 2

I am delighted to include the *The Vibrant Relationship* in this series, as the book, first published in Denmark in 2007 and extremely well received, continues the recent trend to include books that can be easily read by professionals and non-professionals alike because extremely complex ideas are presented in an appealing format that is interesting and easy to read at the same time as being theoretically rigorous and up to date. The design and format of this book, with the use of colour, including the beautiful illustrations of the internationally recognized artist Viktor IV, are a further innovation in the series, but one that ensures that the medium is, indeed, the message. As one Danish reviewer said, "Only rarely does a book fall into your hands that is so inviting and so beautifully illustrated that you feel like giving it to your friends for aesthetic reasons". *The Vibrant Relationship* is such a book.

The aesthetic appeal of the book extends, in my view, to the way in which ideas from many different contemporary models of human development and couple work are elegantly synthesized and presented in a highly readable form. I envisage busy professionals, whose agency remit does not include offering couple therapy, but who, nevertheless, recognize a need for couple therapy as central to the care plan ideally needed for change to occur in a client system, feeling that they have in this book a relevant and attractive resource to offer couples. The book will be invaluable to the many couples who themselves recognize, regardless of their contact with professionals, their need to work on their relationship issues in order for a situation to change. As a resource that couples can use as a source of so-called "self help", working with this text may sometimes mean that professional help is not necessary, or less professional help is needed.

The authors are two of Denmark's most experienced and well-known couple therapists and they have a passion, reflected in the "*vibrant*" of the title, for what can inspire and sustain both professionals and couples as they seek to tackle the sometimes difficult challenges of living and working therapeutically together. The authors share experiences from their journey as a couple and their journeys as therapists, offering a range of rich ideas and skills that can help readers make sense of the sometimes bewildering landscape of relationships and, most importantly, normalize their experiences. In Part 1, the authors introduce readers to a "map" for making sense of the landscape they inhabit and with which they are maybe all too familiar, and in Part 2, the authors offer, as it were, a "virtual tour" with "map" and themselves as guides to places of interest to visit and linger in the landscape when designing and building a vibrant relationship.

Naming the "elephants in the room" by including sections such as *What Are You Carrying In Your Baggage? Your Brain Is A Partner As Well As On Opponent*, and *Conflicts Are Pure Gold*, the authors take readers to the central issue for couples and couples' therapists: how do we manage differences? The authors aim to take the reader beyond the place of simply "managing" differences, and introduce many tried and tested exercises, particularly *The Dialogue of Acknowledgement*, that show couples how differences can be enriching and a cause for celebration. Throughout the book, there are examples of vignettes from couples' lives, emphasizing the transformations that become possible when couples become curious and listen with an acknowledging and appreciative attention to one another's relationship experiences. The landscapes couples inhabit may not change, but they will begin to "see with new eyes". This idea about the way we uncover new options has long been in use in the field of systemic thinking and practice and understood as underpinning the way change occurs in any human system.

This book and its companion volume, *The Vibrant Family*, to be published in this series later in 2011, show once again the importance and relevance of the relational (systemic) paradigm for contemporary society. Twenty-first century research in neuroscience now supports the twentieth century beliefs of therapists that understanding the patterns that connect and the patterns that disconnect promotes brain activity congruent with emotional well-being. Complex ideas are concisely described by the authors, with references to up to date theory and research, and are included in the text in ways that readers interested in connecting the authors' synthesis of ideas with twentieth and twenty-first century developmental psychology, neurobiology, attachment theory, the work of Carl Rogers, and many others, can easily do so.

It is said that in the field of couple therapy, great strides have been made in theory and research in the past twenty-five years, and contemporary society more than ever recognizes the need of support for promoting healing for couple relationships as a mental health issue, and the need to be able to offer ways to do so. This is a book which I hope will be useful, not only because of the windows opened on to contemporary theory and research, but as a practical resource for couples, whether they are wanting to repair their relationship or wanting fresh inspiration for living in their relationship, for professionals working with couples, and for students looking for ways to understand the complex field of couple therapy. At a time such as this, with cutbacks in services, rigid eligibility criteria for access to services, and waiting lists often meaning couple therapy is beyond the reach of many at risk couples who cannot afford to privately fund themselves, I believe this book can be useful as a source of information, encouragement, and practical help.

Ros Draper
Hampshire
2011

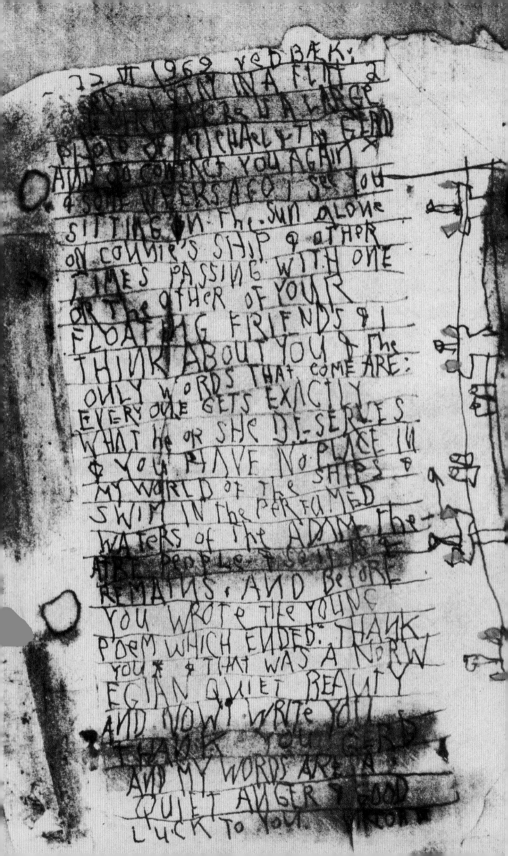

12 II 1969 RØDBÆK:
...I'M IN A FLIT. I
...RATHER CR U A LARGE
PHOTO OF ... MICHAEL I'M GLAD
AND TO CONTACT YOU AGAIN X
4 SOME WEEKS AGO I SEE YOU
SITTING IN THE SUN ALONE
ON CONNIE'S SHIP & OTHER
TIMES PASSING WITH ONE
OR THE OTHER OF YOUR
FLOATING FRIENDS & I
THINK ABOUT YOU & THE
ONLY WORDS THAT COME ARE:
EVERYONE GETS EXACTLY
WHAT HE OR SHE DI-SERVES
& YOU HAVE NO PLACE IN
MY WORLD OF THE SHIPS &
SWIM IN THE PERFUMED
WATERS OF THE ADAM THE-
ABE PEOPLE & SOON BE
REMAINS, AND BEFORE
YOU WROTE THE YOUNG
POEM WHICH ENDED: THANK
YOU X & THAT WAS A NORW
EGIAN QUIET BEAUTY
AND NOW I WRITE YOU
THANK YOU GERD
AND MY WORDS ARE A
QUIET ANGER & GOOD
LUCK TO YOU. VINCENT

PART
1

EnDUriNg and bECOMing

OUR TURNING POINT

C reating and sustaining a vibrant relationship is one of the most difficult challenges we come across in our lives, but when we succeed, it is the source of a truly deep and lasting happiness. To succeed, we need some tools to help us on our way.

The subject of this book is the "Dialogue of Acknowledgement", a loving but extremely efficient tool that can help you to tackle your problems and form the basis for a new way of living and ethical practice, within both your relationship as a couple and all other relationships in life.

We believe that using the Dialogue of Acknowledgement is an excellent way of learning how to interact with others, particularly your partner, with a greater degree of compassion and empathy, thus leading to greater peace of mind. This is a tool that helps us to value other people's reality and take it as seriously as we wish others to take our own. In this way, we do not merely create a more caring atmosphere for our own partner and children, but, in a modest way, we can also contribute to a better and kinder world.

This is a book about opportunities for you to begin and sustain healthy ways of being in your relationship. What we are talking about are small changes with significant effects. So, for example, instead of saying, in the time-honoured way, "My partner must change so that I can develop", we say, "When both of us change we can both develop, and we will be doing it together."

Small changes can, however, often be difficult to make, since we are actually talking about changing habits. For one reason or another, we have adopted the habits we carry in our "baggage", but, in terms of developing the relationship both of you dream about and deserve, these habits are counter-productive. It is important to realize that we have very good reasons for having developed these habits, since they have helped us to survive.

Equally important is that it is not you who will know which of these old habits stand in the way, but your partner, who will tell you. However, the way your partner draws your attention to a habit, often quite spontaneously, can have the effect of making you do it more rather than less.

We hope this book will take you into unfamiliar territory and show you how to do things you are not used to doing, and that these new tools will help you and your partner to develop the vibrant, open, and trusting relationship you want.

NO EASY SOLUTIONS

There is no quick and easy way to a mature, strong, and mindful relationship. The journey consists of small steps towards creating increasing confidence as you learn to counter your old habits, survival strategies, and seemingly uncontrollable emotions. However, part of the process is also discovering the way in which differences can be enriching for your relationship, rather than threatening.

The Vibrant Relationship is not just a book that promotes marriage or relationship *per se*. We think it is an optimistic book about new opportunities that are just within our reach - if we are prepared to make a little effort.

Our contribution to this subject is based on a deep desire to pass on experiences from our own lives, as well as from our many conversations with couples. We use the Dialogue of Acknowledgement in our work, as well as in our personal lives, and the result is that we nearly always see any coldness and dislike dissolve, giving way to new closeness and intimacy. It is an amazing experience when couples reach that moment where, perhaps for the first time in years, they see their partners in a completely new light. At that moment, a couple begins to understand that the disturbing and destructive power struggles or the pain of disconnection can be understood, on a deeper level, as an invitation to growth.

This book is a manual in the true sense of the word. It offers practical advice and important background information for when your relationship is failing or when dreams and vitality are on standby, and can help you get back on track towards making your life together what you hoped it would be at the beginning of your relationship.

Alternatively, if your relationship seems to be functioning well and you just want some new ideas about it, or a new perspective on it, the tools described here will give you increased awareness of your opportunities.

WE HAVE BEEN THERE

In the twenty-five years we have been together, we have spent a lot of time and effort trying to find our way in our relationship. Until almost ten years ago, we did not have an effective means for change in either our professional or our private lives, and our relationship was in crisis. We realized that we needed tools that could not only get us back on track, but also ensure that the closeness, the deep contact, and the nurturing in our relationship would not diminish as the years go by.

Then we came across "Imago Relationship Therapy", which began to influence our love life as well as our working life. We realized that this was an effective way to work with unwanted and wearying disappointments, power struggles, and misunder-standings in the relationship.

In imago relationship therapy, the role of the therapist is to support rather than to guide. This is very much in line with our beliefs about self-help and equality: the couples are the experts on their own lives. The simple tools that the therapy provides make it possible to form a new perspective on the relationship, so that the disconnection and the recurrent power struggles are replaced by a renewed affection and intimacy - in short, love.

This approach is also in line with our views on healing and treatment, since our work as therapists is not based on diagnoses or rigid descriptions of what the treatment should be, but on a non-authoritarian, creative, and respectful way of relating based on equality, where the couples are always the experts on their own lives, and where our role is to elicit the resources which we believe all couples have.

THE DIALOGUE OF ACKNOWLEDGEMENT

Through the Dialogue of Acknowledgement, we gained a completely new understanding of how we could approach our differences with curiosity instead of with scepticism or irritation. Most importantly, it became evident to us that behind every critique and every frustrated wish there is always a constant yearning for something better. Becoming aware of the causes of our frustration has created an entirely new way for us of being together, where we have begun to explore safely the constant challenges to ourselves as individuals and to our shared life.

For these reasons, we undertook additional training in therapy for couples, and this became one of the best and most active experiences in our professional lives in the fields of psychology and psychiatry. Based on our experiences, and inspired by Imago Therapy, we developed the tool we call the "Dialogue of Acknowledgement". It has been adapted to Danish culture and mentality, and consists of conversations that generate new contact and understanding; in other words, of the fulfilling communication we all aspire to and can master.

The Dialogue of Acknowledgement is strongly influenced and informed by:

- Carl Rogers' work on the significance of the unconditional positive regard
- knowledge about the significance of our early attachment patterns
- new brain research, which explores how the brain works, and how emotions are generated
- systemic and narrative thought.

The Dialogue of Acknowledgement is based on the following elements, which will be described in detail in the second part of the book, where practical issues are dealt with:

- acknowledgement
- turn-taking – we take turns in telling our stories
- patient listening
- curiosity and transparency
- re-visioning the future of the relationship.

We have chosen to call our approach the Dialogue of Acknowledgement because acknowledgement and appreciation are the central concepts in our therapeutic work. By acknowledgement, we mean a fundamental approach in which we are able to put ourselves in our partner's shoes and see the world as he or she sees it; by appreciation, we mean affirming the other person's view. Acknowledging requires the capacity to respect the fact that our partner has versions of reality that differ from our own in radical ways. Being different does not mean being wrong. Acknowledging has a fantastic effect: it stimulates and supports further personal growth and development. When your partner acknowledges you, you feel seen, heard, understood, and respected as the person you are. The feeling of peace and security that acknowledgement creates will empower you and your partner to take on the challenge of change in your relationship. Needless to say, your partner's transformation also furthers your own development.

Using the Dialogue of Acknowledgement is not just a temporary process. Once it becomes second nature, it can open the door to a completely new way of being together, not just as a couple, but also with children, friends, and colleagues. We hope it will become a new habit. Seeing, acknowledging, and appreciating the world in this way leads to – if you like – a new ethics of respecting differences, which could be a rich and fruitful soil in which to grow your relationships with the people you hold dear.

In powerful and simple ways, the Dialogue of Acknowledgement, being a reciprocal and caring process, creates a space for the underlying, often painful, stories to emerge, so that we can begin to deal with the effect they have of blocking the joy and vitality that characterize the thriving relationship.

In this book, we would like to share our optimism and demonstrate the opportunities available to couples who want to create understanding and change in their relationships. We wrote it because, now more than ever, we feel and experience our relationship in ways that break through the barriers to love and intimacy. We are certain that we have found the tools to enable us to liberate our own relationship in such a way that our shared life will thrive.

It is our hope that this book will help to introduce you to a shared life of openness, curiosity, acknowledgement, appreciation, and recognition. We want the book to help you learn how to converse and to listen, so that it will be possible for you to explore yourselves and each other in new ways.

This book is for all couples who are looking for new ideas, as well as for couples who feel their relationships are not working, but who, nevertheless, have the desire and the courage to fight for their love in order to get the life we all long for.

STOP THE VICIOUS CIRCLE

We believe that by using this book, couples who are struggling in their relationship can create better conditions for their children.

We often forget that the well-being of the parents is paramount to the well-being of the entire family. The emotional atmosphere between the father and the mother is the air that the children have to breathe. If the pain of the parents pollutes the space, the children have to learn survival strategies in the unsafe, loveless atmosphere.

When parents come to us with a child who is not thriving, we often see symptoms of psychological strain, which are the result of the parents' difficulties. So, children's psychological difficulties are often expressions of tensions and stress in the parental relationship and in the wider family.

Owing to the parents' unresolved problems, the children will not get the necessary help from them to develop beyond the limits which they, the parents, are struggling to overcome. The parents' own development is a decisive factor in the support of their children's development, and we see how many children's symptoms can change if the parents get qualified help to move on in life.

We found that by taking an interest in the love, presence, conflicts, and power struggles in our relationship, we were also caring for our children and their children by not passing on our neglect and painful patterns, which were the consequences of our own parents' neglect.

Kirsten Seidenfaden
and Piet Draiby

OUR RELATIONSHIP IS NOT A PROBLEM TO BE SOLVED. IT IS AN ADVENTURE TO BE LIVED

– HEDY SCHLEIFER –

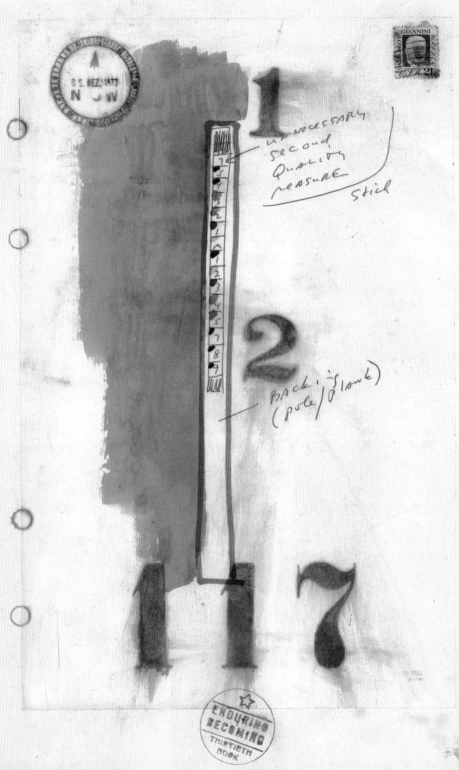

unnecessary
second
quality
measure
stick

backing
(pole/plank)

IT IS NEVER TOO LATE TO HAVE
A GOOD RELATIONSHIP

Why do we suddenly focus our energy on the children, the computer, or our work, instead of developing our relationship with our partner? Why does the loving, sensual woman you knew gradually change into a bad-tempered shrew? Why does the considerate man you knew turn into a bore, a withdrawn uncommunicative caveman who is never at home? And why do we constantly run into the same problems and power struggles in our relationships, no matter how many partners we attempt to settle down with?

There are many different answers to these questions. The most useful one is that we often have no idea how to change the dangerous course of events that all too often end up damaging the love and tearing the relationship apart. If repairing a relationship were as easy as repairing the damage to our roof, we would know how to go about it, but, quite often, we simply have no idea how to patch up our relationship.

So we do nothing at all, even when it is absolutely clear that the relationship is in danger, and even if we know deep down that the precious love between us is slipping away like sand through our fingers.

It is not easy to understand why we do nothing. We are all well aware of the huge drama of going through a separation or a divorce, and the loss experienced by the adults and the children involved. The powerlessness we feel when realizing that it will not be possible to salvage the relationship can be overwhelming. Records show that in approximately 60% of families with children under the age of fourteen, the parents throw in the towel and separate.

It is our conviction that many of these relationships and marriages would survive if the couple received new information about the appropriate tools to get the relationship and the family back on track in the ways described in this book.

PROBLEMS CAN BE SOLVED

It *is* possible to find our way out of the wreck of a capsized relationship. We can free ourselves from the old habits and survival strategies which threaten to destroy many relationships.

Fortunately, it no longer seems to be a taboo to invest time and money in improving and developing our relationships. Many of us realize that in the long run a divorce will not solve our problems. A divorce may lead to a repetition of familiar crises or create a number of new dilemmas.

Nevertheless, it seems difficult to do something about it. Change is painful and rarely comes naturally. Self-development requires courage and stamina.

When wondering what to do, we may question whether "now" is the right time to act. When should we stop beating about the bush and begin to make concrete and practical attempts to restore the energy and the freedom we used to enjoy in our relationship?

Take a look at the statements in the bulleted list below. If you agree with any one of them, you and your partner need to take a closer look at your relationship.

THE REAL VOYAGE OF DISCOVERY
CONSISTS NOT IN SEEKING
NEW LANDSCAPES,
BUT IN HAVING NEW EYES

– MARCEL PROUST –

IT IS THE RIGHT TIME TO TAKE ACTION IF:

- you experience the same quarrelsome discussions over and over again, although you attempt to change the scenario;

- you find yourself in a *quid pro quo* relationship, where an over-scrupulous observance of democratic rights and debating procedures increasingly controls your normal, everyday life;

- you begin to think that your relationship is not a good match and that you have chosen the wrong partner;

- you realize that you are not focusing on your relationship and that you are beginning to devote time and energy to all kinds of other projects;

- your partner repeatedly blames you and criticizes you for investing your energy outside the relationship, although you feel that you have done your best to focus on the relationship;

- you begin clockwatching through the evenings and go to bed half an hour before or after your partner;

- people in your network express concern about your well-being;

- you have greater confidence in your friends than in your partner;

- you notice that your child is not thriving and that you and your partner cannot agree on the right kind of help;

- you begin to feel bored in your relationship and you start spending time with other people;

- you are unfaithful and yet wish to continue in your relationship;

- you feel that your relationship has become too turbulent and violent, and you have run out of ideas as to how to create more harmony and balance;

- you experience symptoms of anxiety, depression, and stress, and want to explore options other than medication;

- you have a problem with substance abuse and you wish to stop self-harming;

- you experience that your differences and disagreements begin to threaten the relationship;

- you and your partner have been exposed to severely traumatizing incidents, such as traffic accidents or the loss of a child, and find yourself emotionally distant from one another.

These statements also apply when your partner mentions any of the above to you, and you vehemently disagree!

JUST ONE TINY SPARK IS ENOUGH

Perhaps you feel that your problems are unique and unsolvable or that there is no hope for a relationship that, for many years, has been a wasteland. The answer is that no matter what problems you may have or what age you are, there is plenty of hope as long as you have preserved a tiny spark of goodwill that can help you counter the difficulties you are experiencing in your relationship.

We had all but thrown in the towel

"Our son was two years old and we had already been divorced for more than a year. Then we tried 'the Dialogue of Acknowledgement' as a last-ditch attempt to bring us together again. The wonderful thing was that we learnt to listen to each other on a very profound and, at the same time, very familiar level. The ability to listen, and especially the feeling of being heard again, had a surprising, liberating, and positive effect.

"It became crystal clear to us that the issues we were arguing about were rarely the dilemma. The real problem was almost always that painful experiences from the past surfaced and came between us. To us, the ground-breaking aspect of the Dialogue of Acknowledgement was the fact that we received some simple tools to help each other heal the wounds of childhood.

"Since then, we have applied the method very often in order to work our way through disagreements, misunder-standings, and hurtful experiences. The method has had a tremendous effect on our relationship, to the extent that we have resolved the mistrust that had built up between us during our time together.

Now we are living together again and are married. We are deeply grateful."

Anne Christine and Anders

MY PARTNER HESITATES

In our counselling of couples, we often find that only one person in the couple has realized that radical action is needed in order to get back on track and restore the previous optimism.

With most of the couples we meet for therapy, we often see that one or the other feels as if he or she has been dragged along. In our own case, Piet was very reluctant to go to our first seminar for couples.

There are many good reasons for couples not being ecstatic about going to therapy. You may perceive it as an admission of failure and a personal defeat to ask a stranger for help. Some men may think, "I'm not going to talk to anyone else. We should be able to deal with this ourselves." Most people in this situation do not have the slightest idea of how to start. Others may be overwhelmed with feelings of shame, guilt, anger, and a sense of injustice.

You may fear being criticized by a therapist, or that the therapist will take sides, implying that you are in the wrong. Will you then have to change?

Probably some of you are afraid that you or your partner might break down if too many hurtful issues are stirred up.

You might also worry that if you reveal emotions and vulnerability, your partner will use this knowledge against you at a later stage. Some of you will say you have neither the time nor the energy to go to therapy to listen to the complaints you have had to put up with for years. Finally, we also meet many couples who, busy fulfilling all their personal ambitions, still have no idea how to begin to change a wrecked relationship and reconnect with their partner.

To the sceptics among you, we would like to emphasize that you do not have to be afraid of the idea of change. The Dialogue of Acknowledgement, quite simply, consists in listening and, when your turn comes, telling your story and being listened to, doing away with the need for a referee, being centre stage, being self-righteous, showing prejudice, humiliation, critique, insistence, or blaming and shaming,

The Dialogue of Acknowledgement, at its core, is a gentle way for you to rebuild confidence in one another. It will enable you to see, hear, and understand each other. That means that you both proceed at your own pace.

It is also of great significance that the course of events is predictable. Participating in the Dialogue of Acknowledgement happens by invitation and appointment, and is not something you do across the dining room table or when you are in a rush and focusing on the need to do something else. It is, thus, more predictable than a conversation. You invite your partner, make an appointment, and reserve some time for the project, until one day this way of being together becomes second nature, so you do not have to follow the script rigidly. You will have discovered how to listen to each other, and to be curious about conflicting interests and differences, instead of confronting the problems with anger or hostility.

In other words, the Dialogue of Acknowledgement aims to liberate you from hurtful habits and survival strategies and, instead, enable you to develop a completely new way of communicating and being together.

Because the Dialogue of Acknowledgement is not a complicated tool, courageous couples who are patient and open will be able to take the process into their own hands and develop their relationship.

Each of the exercises we describe in this book is structured in such a way that it can be carried out without help from a therapist. The exercises should be perceived as opportunities for change. People respond very differently to doing exercises: some are enthusiastic; others prefer to improvise. The process is entirely in your hands. In this way, you have already begun to take responsibility for creating the conditions that will help your relationship to change.

USING THE BOOK

Throughout the book, we use "we" and "you". We share our experiences and invite you and your partner to explore the ideas and try things out together, because only when you share your knowledge with your partner does your relationship develop. We have found that the knowledge and insight we gain as individuals do not usually change the relationship

The Vibrant Relationship is divided into two parts.

In Part I, you will find the background knowledge necessary to understand the Dialogue of Acknowledgement, as well as a description of the most important reasons that so many couples lose their bearings in the relationship. Part I also explains some of the challenges the couple will encounter, from the first infatuation through to the power struggles that no relationship escapes.

There is a detailed account of the reasons why power struggles occur and the stuff of which they are made. Part I ends with a section on brain science. Change is not just related to knowledge about yourself and your partner and how you experience your shared history. Change also involves knowledge about what is going on in your brain in stressful situations. In what follows, we will look at ways for your brain to be your partner, as well as your opponent, in the relationship game.

Part II presents examples of situations in which you can use the Dialogue of Acknowledgement tool. Here, you will also find detailed descriptions of how you set up the dialogue. You will also find examples of how various couples have used this tool, and with what results.

We take a comprehensive look at the positive meaning of conflicts and frustrations. In fact, conflicts are nuggets of gold, waiting to be mined.

We encourage you to work through the exercises together. It might be a good idea to buy a notebook – a logbook of sorts –

where you gather the thoughts that come to mind when you read the book and go through the exercises. There, you can record the new knowledge and insights you get on your journey. New discoveries and insights are volatile knowledge and might be "archived vertically" – forgotten – if we do not make an effort to retain them. A logbook may help you to integrate the new knowledge.

Towards the end of the book, you will find suggestions as to how you might maintain the new knowledge, curiosity, and closeness. There will also be some tips on how you may continue to add vital elements to your love life.

EXERCISES AND SCIENCE

The Vibrant Relationship has colour-coded pages which make it easier to find your way around the book. The colour codes have specific meanings:

- orange contains exercises;
- grey contains relevant theory for anyone interested in the background of the ideas;
- turquoise contains descriptions by couples who have worked with the Dialogue of Acknowledgement.

Any section can be read independently.

If you need more knowledge or want to do more work on your relationship, then you are always welcome to visit the Centre for Relationship Focused Therapy, via www.relationsterapi.dk (English version). There, you will find links and references to lectures, courses, and therapists who work with the Dialogue of Acknowledgement.

Finally, we hope you will enjoy reading this book.

DAN ARCHER

-2. APR. 1972

TO M FORRESTER

ARE WOMEN EVER SATISFIED?

NOT VERY
OFTEN FOR
WOMAN IS
THE LAW

THE NEW AMSTERDAM SCHOOL
OF IKON PAINTING
(SHIPS) D AMSTEL 49 BIJ WATERLOOPLEIN
AMSTERDAM - HOLLAND

97

TWAALFDE BOEK
DAY OF THE SUN

WHY DO WE GET LOST IN LOVE?

Our entire lives are characterized by a longing to experience loving relationships. This is because, on a biological level, human beings were not meant to be alone. In order for human beings to thrive, we need close and intimate relationships, such as the one most of us experience in the first year of our lives.

We do not create meaning on our own; meaning is always created in relationships.

Even when we are virtually on our own, we are always relating to "someone out there", or someone close, because all our experiences are in relation to another. We see ourselves as we are seen by significant others.

By and large, our identity is shaped in the interactions with others, because we continually assess the effect we have on our surroundings and their response to us. For this reason, relationships are the "place" in which human beings are offered the greatest opportunities for growth and development.

THE ONLY THING WE NEVER GET ENOUGH OF IS LOVE, AND THE ONLY THING WE NEVER GIVE ENOUGH OF IS LOVE

– HENRY MILLER –

LONELINESS KILLS!

There is a critical mass of scientific evidence to the effect that there is a positive correlation between health and life expectancy and living in a committed relationship or other relationships. Living in isolation, being lonely, or having a weak social network are risk factors in terms of health. Inability to form satisfactory relationships to significant others and, for example, bullying during childhood, constitute lifelong health risks.

The risk of developing psychological illnesses increases when you lead an isolated life. The conditions involved can among others be frequent episodes of

- depression;
- anxiety;
- sleep disorder;
- symptoms of stress;
- suicidal thoughts;
- other psychological illnesses.

The risk of developing physical illnesses is shown in the literature: there is a connection between loneliness and

- infectious diseases;
- heart and circulatory diseases;
- stomach and intestinal diseases;
- immune system diseases/allergies;
  certain types of cancer.

Of course, life as a single person is not automatically associated with loneliness, and you can also experience loneliness within a relationship (Rholes & Simpson, 2004).

TOGETHER AND APART IS A STRONG UNION

It can be incredibly difficult for two people to agree with one another. The complication is that in order to develop, each person needs to be separate and mature. However, it becomes even more complicated when it is also necessary to be a mature individual in order to develop a harmonious and dynamic relationship. This maturity and secure love is based on a strong definition of self: the fact that we know who we are and what we need from a strong and safe relationship. In the developing intimate relationship we must be able to be close and, at the same time, leave each other in peace. This is also alpha and omega in the relationship between parents and child. The problem arises when one wants closeness and the other needs to be alone, and this pattern is reinforced when conflicts accumulate.

This shows that it is difficult to develop an ability to sustain a deep mutual connection combined with a strong consciousness of one's self. Demographic tendencies show that an increasing number of people abandon the idea of being in a close love relationship and opt instead for a single life.

It is almost taboo to discuss the fact that more than half of us are unable to move from a fulfilling love affair to a sustainable dynamic love. Our view is that one of the best-kept secrets of our day and age is that love, to an increasing number of people, apparently, is experienced only in short intervals that inevitably lead to serial monogamy.

When the heady momentum of the love affair wanes like the moon, we respond with exaggerated urgency to this disturbing loss of love. Instead of bringing an overview of the situation into play, together with new competences, divorce or infidelity become the solutions to the loss of love, the insoluble conflicts, and the lack of contact and intimacy which many couples encounter.

PRESSURE ON THE RELATIONSHIP

We want to make it quite clear that, in a lifelong relationship, love moves through many different phases. Perhaps we meet as young lovers. Later, we may live together for many years, parenting our children. Ideally, we will end our lives as old, loving, and wise partners. Every phase demands a particular insight into the self and respect for the other person's ways of seeing. These phases of love can only develop if the relationship grows in harmony with the stages we go through.

There are quite a few good explanations as to why we so often lose our way in love.

Choosing your partner with your heart only became common practice around 100 years ago, so, historically speaking, we are pure amateurs in the art of marrying and living together out of love. Prior to that time, decisions about whom you spent your life with were based on family choice and societal beliefs. It was only in the twentieth century, when the free choice of partner became generally accepted, that love and devotion became decisive issues in this process.

In an overall perspective, therefore, it is not automatic that we should be in a close relationship with another human being. Research into the human ability to form attachments shows that more than 40% of us experience great difficulties in forming an adult attachment to another human being in a secure and confident way. When our way of connecting with others is disturbed in infancy, it can affect our ability to accept and give love in adulthood, because closeness seems disturbing and unsafe. This important subject is one of the pivotal points of the book.

Contemporaneously with the free choice of a partner, the nuclear family structure of a mother, a father, and children emerged, a structure that is only about 120 years old. Finally, it is only since about fifty years ago that we have had the possibility of getting a divorce at our disposal, if we felt that love had died or we found someone else. So, it is perfectly understandable that in our day and age we fumble around in the dark trying to find a more ideal way to live together – in love.

We would say that if we have a long relationship, perhaps lasting for a lifetime, we would go through many relationships with the same partner, because we change as human beings and because each phase of the relationship makes new and profound demands on us.

The relationship and the family are affected by "the signs of the times" in so far as they are presently under colossal pressure. We live in an age of excessive expectations, pressures, and demands concerning education, work, happiness, money, love, children, and family. The pressures and demands are cumulative, making it even more difficult to be in a relationship because we are constantly deflected and distracted from our focus on the relationship in our quest to achieve it all – preferably now, at once.

We want everything to be picture-perfect and beat ourselves and one another up, when we do not achieve this goal. We harbour unrealistically high ideals and expectations of life, defined by the *Zeitgeist* and ourselves. Expectations, inculcated in our childhood, are also part of our emotional baggage. What should I be like as a mother or a father, as a wife or a husband, what should our home and family be like, and what about my working life, my friends, and my body?

The perspective on life that the Western world has embraced for many years is constantly putting the spotlight on us: our individual needs, limits, opportunities, and development. It is a lifestyle with the clear objective that you should personally achieve as much as possible in your individual life: a brilliant career, a top salary, and a wonderful house, complete with a large family car with room for many children. All this tells the world at large that *you know how to have a good life and be happy.*

In our view, we have reached a point where we can no longer pretend not to be aware of the fact that this individualistic rat-race has led to an emotional desert, where love and other life-giving relationships between people are suffering from extremely unfavourable growth conditions. Incredible amounts of stress and a never-ending battle against diseases resulting from one's lifestyle speak for themselves: the consumption of alcohol, sleeping pills, and pharmaceuticals such as Prozac, with which we attempt to regulate our unmanageable emotions, continue to break each previous year's records.

During the development of our individualistic lifestyle, we, to some extent, abandon the conventional frameworks of family and love-life, time-honoured institutions where couples have traditionally found support when facing difficulties.

In previous times, and in many contemporary cultures, there was and is a moral, cultural, and a religious framework that offers guidance as to how you should live your life. With the best of intentions, we have now, in the name of personal freedom, done away with all traditional authorities without replacing them. This means that many of us get trapped in chaotic lifestyles, characterized by no particular supportive customs, practices, or traditions. Furthermore, a strong emphasis on twosomeness and family is often lacking. It is in situations like this that we can often use the Dialogue of Acknowledgement to explore what we actually want from each other and what kind of life we really want to have together. We – children and adults alike – need to take time out and talk about the most important issues in terms of our well-being and happiness.

In this day and age we are, for better or worse, left to our own devices when it comes to mapping the territory and creating solutions as to how we want to live our lives. This leaves many of us stranded between a rock and a hard place.

WE ARE BORN IN CONNECTION
WE SUFFER IN SOLITUDE
WE DEVELOP IN RELATION

– ANNE-LISE LØVLIE SCHIBBYE –

RESEARCH INTO RELATIONSHIPS

The American researcher John Gottman has undertaken probably the longest continuous analyses of the hinterlands of hearts and relationships. For twenty-eight years he has observed more than 3000 couples and made more than thirty different studies. By focusing specifically on emotionally intelligent couples, he found that they resembled each other in seven fundamental ways.

Gottman's seven principles for a viable long-term relationship are:

1. knowledge about each other's worlds;

2. actively experiencing joyful admiration of the other (the best antidote against anger);

3. facing each other instead of turning away;

4 allowing your partner to influence you;

5. solving the solvable problems;

6. overcoming deadlocks;

7. creating shared worlds.

On the basis of this research, John Gottman has shown he can predict divorce with more than 95% accuracy. He describes four "apocalyptic horsemen" in a relationship: criticism, contempt, defence, and stonewalling, which lead to considerable frustration and predict an imminent divorce. Gottman further points out that we must be aware that 70% of our marital problems cannot be solved! We must, in other words, learn to live with them in advantageous ways . . . (Gottman, 1999).

WE ARE AT A CROSSROADS

The Dialogue of Acknowledgement described in this book is an extremely efficient way of pointing you in certain directions and introducing some tools that can help you and your partner develop.

In addition, the Dialogue of Acknowledgement represents a new way of communicating, and a new set of rules to live by, so this approach is more than a tool designed for couples in crisis. These rules constitute an ethic of how to exist in the world, an ethic that breathes new life into the emotional atmosphere and creates an open and loving way to be together. This is the sort of emotional environment we can offer our developing children.

This new awareness is perfectly in line with the way that developmental psychology now looks at the important influence of our relations with our significant others. Now the contemporary therapies are focusing on approaches where our relationships with others are central (relational therapy). This does not mean rejecting the intrapsychic way of thinking about and doing therapy. The most popular new approaches can each be traced back to earlier approaches to therapy. The intrapsychic model is a laboriously constructed, solid edifice built on the foundations of classical psychology, with the belief that growth and development rely on insights and understanding of the individual's past and present needs.

If we only focus on ourselves – my needs, dreams, desires, limits, or hardships, my childhood, my parents, my success or my working life – then we will very soon get sidetracked. In such a situation it will be difficult for us to see that the family, the marriage, and the close relations are the source of the quality of life and the happiness many of us long for and strive to attain.

This sidetracking consists in believing that insight into, and understanding of, individual development automatically change our behaviour in the close relationship.

WE BELIEVE IN THE SIGNIFICANCE OF THE INTIMATE RELATIONSHIP

It is our firm belief that this understanding, in time, will become much more generally accepted. The reason is very simple.

No parents, educators, or psychiatrists would, in this day and age, begin to doubt that children have the best chance of a harmonious development if they form confident and secure bonds to significant empathic carers who communicate clearly. Plenty of research demonstrates conclusively that growing up in this kind of emotional environment will have a decisive positive influence on a child's self-esteem and personality. This can also be measured in the development of the brain function, and in the brain chemistry that controls whether or not we are at ease with ourselves and others.

We might ask if the effects, as well as the ways, of all these processes should cease just because we reach adulthood. It is our belief that we adults need the same conditions in order to thrive and express ourselves. In general, we are at our best when we live in a confident, secure, open, and loving relationship.

SHARING THE JOURNEY OF LIFE

Integrating the mindset of the Dialogue of Acknowledgement in our daily lives will take us on a journey in which we move away from habitual behaviours that are hurtful to our partner. The Acknowledging Dialogue will also help us to aim at a more nurturing, acknowledging, and appreciative intimacy. It is a journey that gives us insight into what *triggers* us, to the extent that, in a matter of seconds, we can transform into young, hurt, unreasonable children. The journey will also provide knowledge about the ways in which our triggered reactions cause our partners to experience our communication negatively, which, in turn, affects our relationship for the worse. On this journey of discovery, we gain a full understanding of our mutual responsibility for the quality of the intimacy of our love-life. This responsibility inevitably translates into a deeper awareness of the decisive influence we have on the growth and development of our significant others, just like when we make love or share the passion of dancing a tango.

AFGEGEVEN 2 4 JAN. 1971

C A R T OO N
R O U G H

THE NEW AMSTERDAM SCHOOL
OF IKON PAINTING
(SHIPS) T/O AMSTEL 49 BIJ WATERLOOPLEIN
AMSTERDAM - HOLLAND

IMAGO RELATIONSHIP THERAPY

Imago Relationship Therapy is an approach to Relationship Therapy for couples developed during the 1980s in America by Harville Hendrix and Helen La Kelly Hunt.

Imago is the Latin word for image, and in this context it refers to the earliest experiences of love. We bring these images with us into the relationship.

The basic idea behind Imago Relationship Therapy is that we develop through dialogue with our partner. The approach is based on a particular kind of dialogue that aims to develop new and more appropriate patterns of communication and behaviour, thereby making each of us aware of the significance of our own survival strategies.

The Imago approach is inspired by various psychological theories about how our personality develops in the relationships with our significant others who nurtured and cared for us during our childhood and youth. Survival strategies develop between parents and children, and these strategies imprint themselves on the patterns we apply when entering into close relationships later in life.

According to Imago Relationship Therapy, we fall in love when we meet a partner who incorporates the inner image, the "imago", which we all carry around within us. It is an image which embodies our early childhood experiences, emotions, and ideas. The "imago" also includes those aspects of our personalities that have been repressed. As adults, we may become aware of how we try to compensate for these repressed aspects of our personalities. In Imago Relationship Therapy, this is the basis of the idea that we fall in love with a partner who embodies those aspects of our personalities and competences that we repressed in childhood.

In Imago Relationship Therapy, the therapist has a facilitating role, as it is through the dialogue that the development of the couple and the relationship takes place (Hendrix, & LaKelly Hunt, 2004).

CARL ROGERS

Carl Rogers – often called the quiet revolutionary of psychology – holds our interest because he has comprehensive practical and research based experience in the field of unconditional affirmative therapy, working with individuals, couples, and groups. He was also the first psychotherapist who subjected his theories to scientific testing.

Carl Rogers created his method in 1951, and called it Client-Centred Therapy. With this approach, Carl Rogers distinguished himself clearly from the two previous psychological waves: psychoanalysis and behaviourism. For this reason, Carl Rogers mainly represents the third wave – humanistic or positive psychology – in which the main preoccupation is with factors that shape well-rounded, mature individuals, characterized by an infinite potential for development.

Client-Centred Therapy is based on the hypothesis that human beings, by virtue of their "natural inclination", will develop or "actualize" in the most positive, constructive, creative, and socially proactive direction possible under the given circumstances and conditions. This does not mean that human beings do not have destructive potential. Carl Rogers and the entire humanistic psychological tradition have been terribly misunderstood in this respect. Essentially, it means that the conditions under which human beings grow up and live influence whether or not such destructive forces are engendered.

Carl Rogers' three core conditions for therapy have left a substantial footprint on the landscape of psychotherapy.

1. The therapist must show an unconditional positive approval and appreciation of the client.
2. The therapist must demonstrate an empathetic understanding of the client.
3. The therapist must create a situation where there is concordance between the experience described and authentic communication.

Rogers believed that these three core prerequisites are not only necessary, but also sufficient conditions for the constructive unfolding of the client's potential (Rogers, 1961).

THE RELATIONAL ETHIC

Acknowledging communication is an expression of an attitude towards others that allows us to see our differences without having to fight about who is right or wrong. It is a relational attitude, which we feel could be applied in all areas of life. It is an ethic that allows all members of the community to feel acknowledged and, thereby, have their self-esteem and self-confidence boosted.

This is not about constantly showing acknowledgement and/or giving praise, nor does it focus exclusively on positive issues. Acknowledgement means a willingness to see the world through someone else's eyes for a while, thus enabling the other person to feel that his or her picture of the world makes sense – that he/she is not alone. When we do this, we are showing the responsibility we all have to contribute to the growth and development of our significant others. We have a choice, and this choice of doing – or not doing – is at the core of our sense of the relational ethical choice.

Does it matter? some might ask. Yes, actually, it means everything, since the acknowledgement offers me the opportunity to experience security, growth, and creativity. The Dialogue of Acknowledgement is an example of how a relational ethics can function in practice. In the first instance, your family, your partner, and you yourself may experience the benefits of this approach. Later, everyone you meet on your path through life will benefit.

Acknowledgement is always a two-way process. We only learn something new about ourselves in encounters with people who are different from us. This is where the "struggle for recognition" begins, according to the German philosopher Axel Honneth. Discoveries come about through confrontation followed by reciprocal acknowledgement Thus, differences form the starting point for the struggle, the acknowledgement, and the new insights. Each person is capable of changing his or her own views, in turn influencing others with new ideas. One cannot demand acknowledgement, but one can contribute to the acknowledgement by the way one is present or not in the relationship with the person who is acknowledging you. Thus, we are responsible for creating relationships based on acknowledgement.

We are also responsible for ensuring that "the other" has a sufficient and safe space so that his/her story can unfold, however strange it may seem to us.

The Dialogue of Acknowledgement is a tool that enables us to regain our composure, self-respect, and self-reliance after a relational setback.

On a basic level, the development of our identity can be said to depend on acknowledgement. A human being needs to be seen by others, otherwise he or she becomes invisible. Without acknowledgement, we experience contempt and may feel threatened by loss of personality. A precondition of being able to be ourselves is, therefore, that each of us knows our worth through the acknowledgement of others. We cannot assert our own worth by ourselves; recognition and acknowledgement is given to us by our significant others. Of course, we are all connected in a network of relationships and, in some respects, we would assert that a relational ethic should be self evident. What can ethics possibly be if not relational?

However, since we do find it necessary to talk about a relational ethic, it is partly in order to remind each other that we are constantly engaged in a reciprocal process of co-creating the world in which we live. We say partly because, in our work, we constantly experience how Dialogues of Acknowledgement create change, joy, and intimacy.

Finally, a new consensus is emerging in developmental psychology and neurobiology, pointing to the fact that the individual's potential for development in decisive ways depends on, and is actually decided by, the nature of the relationships in which he/she participates creatively. As described by Løgstrup, individual encounters in our everyday lives also demonstrate that we are profoundly interdependent on each other.

Hence, it is vital that we have a shared Relational Ethic (Honneth, 1996).

ENTHUSIASM

AS COMPASS DIRECTION

AANGFMAAND 1 6 JUNI 1971

THE NEW AMSTERDAM SCHOOL

YES

ONE

YES AND NO

½ — ½

ZERO

NO

in the search for direction which is the process of navigation in
steering pasts the rocks of choice to the harbor of law
there is no magnetic compass
other than the inner feeling of enthusiasm and that is
the only compass and the alert navigator will steer his
course towards the enthusiasm
and good luck

THE LOGBOOK
OF THE SHIP
"HENRY DAVID THOREAU"

88

25C
NEDERLAND

THE EVOLUTIONARY SPIRAL
OF RELATIONSHIPS

W hat goes wrong when two people who are head over heels in love end up killing each other – at least verbally? In order to answer this question, we must first of all go on a grand tour of the mysterious processes of falling in love and developing a relationship. Relationships evolve in a continuously changing spiral (see Figure 1, p. 47).

First, we fall in love, which for some people is an engrossing and all-consuming condition, where everything is possible. We are possessed by the indescribably wonderful feeling of having found the person with whom we can be ourselves, and with whom we feel seen, heard, and loved.

But, sadly, no love affair lasts forever. In time, a number of power struggles emerge in every single love affair. We use the term power struggle to refer to the disagreements and quarrels in our everyday lives, where the differences of the two partners become evident. When we are caught up in power struggles, we feel that love drifts away from us as predictably as a lilo caught by an offshore wind. This prompts some of us to find escape routes out of the relationship – engaging in extramarital affairs, drinking too much, or taking refuge in parallel lives – living separate lives together. Still others choose to throw in the towel and slam the door on the relationship. However, there is also the possibility that the two of you together seek knowledge, new understandings, new ways of being together, and, thereby, move beyond the power struggles to co-create a vibrant relationship.

The characteristics of the vibrant relationship are:

- the well-being of your partner is just as important as yours;
- you express your love every day in many different ways;
- you have learned to create a secure and confident environment for your partner;
- frustrations stimulate curiosity and development;
- you consciously practise and coach yourselves in the art of increasing the intimacy, the passion, the contact, and the communication;
- you help the other to realize his or her dreams and full potential.

The relationship spiral can be divided into two phases:

The love affair and the power struggles can be described as the impulsive and reactive phase, because it is characterized by spontaneous and instinctive responses: we respond, as it were, on autopilot, i.e., on the basis of previous knowledge and experiences.

Beyond the power struggle is the thoughtful and reflective phase, where we apply and develop the ability to listen, using empathy, acknowledgement, and appreciative behaviour in order to grow and develop as individuals and as a couple.

FIGURE 1.
THE EVOLUTIONARY SPIRAL OF RELATIONSHIPS

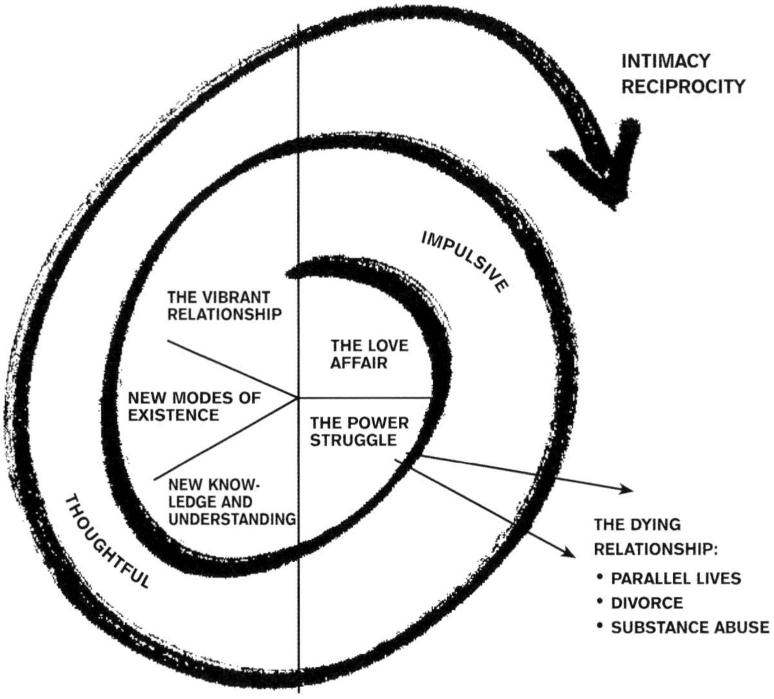

INTIMACY
RECIPROCITY

IMPULSIVE

THE VIBRANT
RELATIONSHIP

THE LOVE
AFFAIR

NEW MODES OF
EXISTENCE

THE POWER
STRUGGLE

NEW KNOW-
LEDGE AND
UNDERSTANDING

THOUGHTFUL

THE DYING
RELATIONSHIP:
• PARALLEL LIVES
• DIVORCE
• SUBSTANCE ABUSE

Source: *Couples Imago Weekend Manual*, developed from Seidenfaden and Simon (2003).
Inspired by, and translated from, Harville Hendrix, PhD (1979).
Getting the Love You Want. Workshop Manual, revised December 1999.

THE MYSTERY OF FALLING IN LOVE AND SELECTING A PARTNER

Most of us have experienced the joy of closeness, the fantastic and inexplicable things that happen during the first euphoric phase of a love affair. You experience the wonderful sensation of not just being *"me"*, but the feeling of being *"we"* in a close union, which seems to fulfil all the needs you could ever imagine. The world opens up and everything is possible. You complement each other, so together you are stronger. A life without the other is inconceivable. In short, you have found your *soul mate*.

In the passion of infatuation, it feels as if we have a perfect match and think alike: It is as if we have known each other forever.

We know that for others a love affair can be more troublesome.

Is it more than a happy coincidence that we find someone who is able to make us feel complete? Or is this experience merely the imagination running wild during this phase that could be described as the monumental madness of being in love?

Why are we attracted to a certain person and not to someone else? Is it at all possible to describe, understand, and explain in scientifically feasible terms what is perhaps the most intense, mind-blowing, and wonderful event in a human life? Should we go ahead and explore it at all, or would it make more sense to let our choice of partner remain one of life's major conundrums?

We think that we should dive in and attempt to investigate what lies behind our choices. Not in order to minimize the beauty of falling in love, body, mind, and soul, but because we will be able to gain new knowledge from better understanding this phase of the relationship life. This knowledge will enable us to become better at optimizing our growth and development in the relationship. We will benefit immensely from this process, as will any children who may be born to us.

When we look at the current research and theories on the choice of partner, we are confronted by many unanswered questions.

The data from recent research suggests enormous and complex interplay between many different factors. Our understanding of the process is still so new that we can as yet only talk about some tendencies in a territory that has not yet been fully mapped.

PIECES IN A GIANT PUZZLE

In the following, we would like to give a description of some of the pieces in the "partner selection puzzle".

Attraction and love are influenced by:

- availability;
- social equality;
- difference.

Being near each other – whether in a classroom or in the neighbourhood – as well as having a certain social, economic, and educational equality, are two significant preconditions of the game.

At the same time, we are attracted by difference on the psychological and behavioural levels. We are infatuated with qualities of a partner which we feel we do not possess ourselves.

This was evident when we fell in love. Kirsten grew up in an environment characterized by rigid rules, where it was considered proper for children to sit nicely, not move too much, keep their elbows off the table, and be seen but not heard. Kirsten fell in love with Piet, whose upbringing was different; he was encouraged to use his body in sports and scouting. Kirsten was attracted to Piet, because he, among other things, had developed aspects that she had repressed.

During this first phase when we are in love, we idealize certain aspects of our partner, which we later experience as negative characteristics.

During our love affair, I felt relieved and happy that Kirsten loved me to the extent that she could guess my innermost feelings. I was mad about her sensitive antennae. However, when the humdrum of everyday life returned, I was not always pleased to find that she could read me like a book. I began to feel that Kirsten's empathy was invasive and manipulating.

Piet

Finally, there is also the pattern that can be described as *I love those who love me!*

The areas of research that presently seem to be most productive in terms of understanding our choice of partner are:

- evolutionary theory (research into human behaviour with a focus on the survival of the species);
- attachment theory (research into early experiences and their formative significance in terms of initiating, developing, and ending close relationships);
- research into the significance of the relations between human beings, as opposed to a focus on individual aspects;
- neurobiological research.

THE BIOCHEMISTRY OF BEING IN LOVE

When we are in love, a certain love potion is produced in the brain. It consists of, among other things, the signal substances dopamine and serotonin, and the hormone noradrenaline.

In later years, research has focused on this area, particularly dopamine, since it is one of the body's natural "happiness hormones". Dopamine is released in large doses when we are in love, but is also released in smaller portions when we eat, have sex, exercise, and do yoga, or when we feel moved or experience intellectual challenges.

Dopamine is also released when we smoke, drink coffee or alcohol, eat chocolate, or take narcotic drugs.

Dopamine makes you feel good. However, the dosage and the way it is released are of vital importance to our relationships. If we have a lot of dopamine in our bloodstream, we are swept off our feet, we do not feel hungry, we only need a few hours of sleep, and we tend to act spontaneously and uncharacteristically. Suddenly, we see ourselves do things we would never do under "normal" circumstances.

Such is the rush of being in love, similar in nature to the intoxication of cocaine and a "runner's high", when dopamine circulates in our system. This is the biochemical explanation of why being in love is one of the most powerful experiences in a human life.

Can you become dependent on dopamine and on being in love? Yes, in a way. Once you are in love with a person, you become increasingly dependent on that relationship. We experience an increasing interdependence, even withdrawal symptoms. We have all experienced being beside ourselves because we had to be away from our sweetheart for a couple of days. And who has not, as some love junkies do, travelled far and wide just for one kiss or a single night?

Like Don Juan, they flit like a butterfly from one flower to the next, continually seeking this particular type of emotional rush.

Perhaps we can *also* begin to understand Don Juan as a reaction to a dependence. With the waning of the love affair, it is as if the effect of the high dose of dopamine is wearing off, maybe reflecting a new tolerance. Perhaps there are good reasons why nature has not given us access to still higher doses!

THE BIOCHEMISTRY OF MATURE LOVE

In the long-term relationship, the cocktail of chemical substances circulating in the brain and the body is different.

When you begin to go steady, and the emotional storms of the love affair have died down, the balance changes between dopamine and the hormones oxytocin in women and vasopressin in men.

The assumption is that high levels of oxytocin/vasopressin in both partners in a relationship ensure that they stay together beyond the first mad rush of the love affair.

Vasopressin supports the complex development of devotion.

Oxytocin and vasopressin influence our ability to bond permanently with the other person. It is released into the body and makes us feel good, for instance, when we receive a hug or are touched.

Testosterone also plays a major part, since it has a significant influence on the desire for sex – which is normally part of a love affair. Later, the testosterone subsides to "normal" levels, which, in most cases, means that men and women have *different* levels of testosterone. Typically, men have higher levels of testosterone than women.

When we know that differences in the levels of hormones and desire are normal, there is no basis for criticism of the partner on this issue.

This is some of the biochemical background information that may explain much of the drama that characterizes the transition to the next phase of the relationship. At this point, other differences (which may have been there all the time) emerge in the humdrum of everyday life.

NO UNIVERSAL ANSWERS

We do not imagine that this background of biochemical information outlined above explains everything. As human beings, we are more than systems only determined by hormones. To us, sexuality is characterized by a complexity that goes beyond all biological models. It is also a multi-faceted interaction between body and soul as well as culture and society, where science is often at a loss.

We have chosen to include this section, not as an explanation, but in order to expand our understanding of some of the most powerful experiences we may have as human beings. We are, so to speak, beginning to translate the "language" of the brain (Love, 2001).

THE POWER STRUGGLE BEGINS

The distinguishing characteristics of couples who succeed in establishing a long-term relationship and the couples who separate are the ways in which they manage power struggles.

Unfortunately, all too many couples do not move beyond this phase. Gradually, their love project seems increasingly remote because, in a manner of speaking, it never escapes from the grip of the iron fist of the power struggles.

As long as we are in love, everything is fine and easy to handle. We can do things we had forgotten we could. Furthermore, we discover abilities we had no idea we possessed. Everything in life seems to go swimmingly.

However, when the first phase of the relationship, the love affair, begins to wane, the gilt is off the gingerbread and is gradually replaced by something much more complex and demanding. We enter a phase that we call the *power struggle*. This is a struggle where we keep on attempting to change each other and we fight repeatedly about whose version of reality is the right one.

The power struggle can be about anything. What is the appropriate time to pick up John from the day nursery? How often is it OK to go out with your friend without your partner? How big an overdraft is OK? What is an acceptable level of mess in our apartment? How often should we see our families? Is it OK to leave hair and toothpaste in the bathroom plug-hole?

The cumulative effect of any of these struggles is that we no longer feel quite so secure with our partner. Nor do we experience the same intense receptivity that characterized the beginning of the relationship, where both of us felt seen, heard, and appreciated like never before.

The power struggles can be overt or more hidden. Whether the conflicts take place openly or beneath the surface, they are caused by our ignorance. We simply do not know how to handle the emotions unleashed in our disagreements and conflicts. Whether we turn into cavemen or shrews, love changes from a wonderful feeling of sharing and harmony to a life where we each do our own thing. When this happens, we realize that there are suddenly a number of needs, experiences, and emotions that we no longer share with each other. In this type of existence, we no longer pay attention to each other and we tend to stop caring for each other.

In this phase, our perception of self and others also changes. Most of us have probably seen or experienced how a consuming delight and love of a partner's behaviour slowly but surely is replaced by irritation, criticism, perhaps even hatred. You may, for example, suddenly begin to criticize your partner's extrovert and gregarious behaviour towards other people, which you fell for and found fascinating, contagious in a big way, when you first met.

Finally, one day we quietly register that our lover or partner is a greater challenge than we had anticipated. It seems that the love between us is running out, to the extent that we no longer have anything to offer each other. Or it may be that the differences between us have increased and that neither of us feels able to bridge the gap any longer.

A once vigorous and effervescent love is now glazed over with indifference. The energy and the romance have slipped out of the back door and are now invested in work and other activities. When we get to this stage, we can choose between saying goodbye to the power struggles and the relationship, or entering the doorway to discover a true love in the Vibrant Relationship.

Escape routes out of the relationship come in many varieties, including the less well-known types. Some couples immediately choose to go to court and solve the problem by getting a divorce. Other couples transfer their energy to their job or an extra-marital affair, and still others react by falling into depression or substance abuse.

Another escape route is the parallel existence, where, by and large, we live separate lives without intimate contact with each other in the same house. One day we might suddenly hear the words, "I have lost interest in you", or "I have found someone else."

OPEN
LOCK
FROM
UNDER
Drawer
NUMBER ONE
the FIRST
WORKTABLE
WORK
SPACE
"A"
Step Benedicta
post in Bristol Riv.
47 Amsterdam
28 April 1976

WE WERE ONCE SO CLOSE

Why and how do we get into these power struggles? Why is it that the disappointments, the resignation, and the hurt about who gets to do what are the only things we talk about?

The truth is very rarely that love has run out, or that one of us has changed, or deliberately hidden less sympathetic qualities from the other.

The criticism and power struggles that occur naturally during the first years of a loving relationship are, in our view, an expression of unresolved emotional issues from childhood which are now gradually coming to the surface.

During crises – whether between lovers, parents, children, or friends – we almost automatically repeat some of the ways in which we learnt to protect ourselves as children, when we lived with our parents and siblings.

This is the trench warfare scenario. Every time a conflict is under way, the cannons are positioned. Entrenched and armed to the teeth, we allow the old survival strategies to run the show. This is the explanation of why an apparently tiny, innocent tiff in no time becomes a major catastrophe. It is also the reason why all too many conversations end with the partners blaming each other, unable to hear the underlying reasons behind the tirades the other is delivering with a vengeance. We take every utterance made in the heat of the battle so personally that we lose our bearings completely; our self-esteem is packed off to Timbuktu, and the old habits surface.

We can also hide in the trenches, conducting a cold war by stonewalling.

The good news is that there is no reason to panic. In fact, it is a natural development which all couples go through in one way or another. All couples move from being in love to engaging in power struggles that, on the surface, look like everyday occurrences.

What we do not register, feel, and understand when we are in the midst of power struggles and fights with our partner is the following.

- Behind our partner's criticism there is a frustration and behind that a longing, which is possibly related to the person's unmet childhood needs.
- When we become insecure and feel pressured, we resort to our old survival strategies.

LEAVING THE RELATIONSHIP THROUGH THE BACK DOOR

It is our wedding anniversary and we are returning by car from a stay at a spa. During recent months, I have requested adjustments and a shared vision of our relationship. However, my husband Christian has withdrawn from this discussion and I cannot stand the situation any longer. In a shaking voice, I ask what he thinks about the two of us on our seventh wedding anniversary.

"Our anniversary is a joke," he says, in an irritated manner.

My heart sinks: "We got married because we damned well wanted to be together!"

Turning the steering wheel, Christian overtakes another car, saying, "We should have got to know each other better before we got hitched."

"But our intentions were excellent," I tell the passing cars, while the safety belt suddenly seems too tight. Christian begins to say that we have nothing in common and that he has failed. I feel a chill and begin to curse, and end by saying that we could hardly be in a worse situation. He agrees.

The famous seven-year crisis has arrived with a vengeance.

Lone

WE DO NOT ACHIEVE CLOSENESS BY BEING RIGHT

One of the main reasons that power struggles occur is the fear of differences that many of us have. For this reason, many of us try to change our partner.

We encounter differences all the time, but when we meet them in an intimate space we each bring our own ways of negotiating them, be they concerned with bringing up the children, how to spend money, sexual desire, or whether or not to have Laura Ashley cushions on the sofa.

Often, our reactions to our partner contribute to the escalation of a conflict that is just lurking under the surface, or to confirming that it is my partner who has to change. So, for example, when either of us insists that now is the time to have a constructive talk about money, or what we do when the kids do not want the food that is served, or the desire to avoid withdrawal into the trenches, when our partner's passion looms large on the horizon.

Over time, many couples experience that it is precisely the differences that once made us feel complete together which gradually turn into irritations, alienation, or contempt.

We are afraid of the differences and the feelings they generate. Many of us believe that if only you think alike and agree on various issues, then life would be much easier. However, there is a "you" and a "me", two strong and different individuals, which never ever should or could have the same thoughts, because we are all different. Believing that we can happily agree on everything is an illusion that comes at a great price. We get into trouble when we, as partners in the relationship, believe we not only should not be different, but also think we are able to guess the other person's thoughts and wants because we know each other inside out.

We believe that it is only when we understand that we are different and are able to move from tolerating our differences to celebrating them without fear that we can reap the fruits and the full potential and generosity of love.

FURTHER NOTES TO SOCIAL WORKERS:

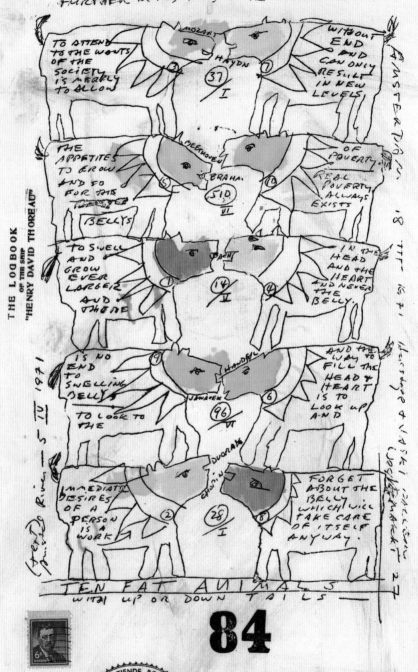

TEN FAT ANIMALS
WITH UP OR DOWN TAILS —

84

WHAT ARE YOU CARRYING IN
YOUR BAGGAGE?

W hen a couple have, for some time, been fighting ruth-
less battles about who is right about what, blaming
each other, and untiringly and unsuccessfully have
attempted to change the other, then they may decide to separate.
Typically, happiness is then pursued in a new relationship, which
all too often ends with the repetition of the same kind of battles.
Alternatively, a couple may choose to stay together and live
parallel lives devoid of passion.

The dismal statistics speak for themselves. More than fifty per cent
of all couples fail to solve their problems. In families with children up to the age of fourteen years, the despair and the frustration
take their toll and more than sixty per cent file for a divorce.

Based on our lifelong experience, we think this is a bad solution.
Many of those couples may actually want a life together; they just
cannot work out how to get back together. Our therapeutic work
with couples shows in convincing ways that it is possible for
partners to find each other again.

The majority of frustrations in the relationship is not related to
the couple and their present life together. They concern the
unresolved conflicts each of them carries along in their baggage
from early childhood and adolescence. Usually, we cannot see
this baggage ourselves. However, gradually, our partners become
aware of the baggage, and, as time goes by, each partner begins to
"trip over the other person's baggage". The influence of our
baggage is such that we believe we are "right".

We look at the world through the spectacles we have created for
ourselves from our childhood. Any couples who make the
conscious decision to unpack their baggage and, thereby, explore
the meanings of the conflicts, the differences, the frustrations,
the rejections, as well as the emotional bruises, create an
opportunity for themselves to set out on a new and exciting phase
in their relationship.

We believe the baggage that we carry with us from childhood into
adult life can be explored and understood using the following
constructs:

- our experiences of nurture;
- our strategies for survival;
- our attachment behaviour (see Chapter Five);
- our adaptation of the self (see Chapter Five);
- the neurobiology of our brain (see Chapter Six).

OUR EXPERIENCES OF NURTURE

What we mean by nurture is our experiences of being cared for during infancy and childhood. Baggage from our infancy and childhood are needs that our parents or others, for one reason or another, were unable to fulfil: needs such as our desire to be seen and heard with the emotions and thoughts we had as children, and our experiences of being cared for by those near and dear to us.

Painful longings and unmet needs run deep, because the habitual patterns of behaviour between child and adult have been repeated, it seems, forever. As time goes on these habitual patterns become integrated into our personality to the extent that we are not conscious of how these longings still control how we behave as adults.

OUR RELATIONSHIPS LIVE IN "THE SACRED SPACE IN BETWEEN". THE MEANING IS TO BE FOUND NEITHER IN ONE OF THE TWO PARTNERS NOR IN BOTH OF THEM TOGETHER, BUT ONLY IN THE ACTUAL DIALOGUE IN THIS "BETWEEN" IN WHICH THEY LIVE TOGETHER.

– MARTIN BUBER –

THE ICEBERG OF EXPERIENCE

Our cumulative experiences and the emotions associated with them can be compared to an iceberg. Only one tenth of an iceberg is visible above the surface of the water. This tenth consists of the experiences and emotions we can "see", feel physically, perceive with our psyche, and describe.

Under "the surface" the unconscious makes up nine tenths. It is here that by far the major part of our experiences and emotions converge. This is where we store the foundations of many of the values, attitudes, and convictions about life that were imprinted upon us as children and adolescents by our parents, friends, teachers, etc.

Here, we find the values and foundations of why we live as we do in healthy or unhealthy ways, single or in couples, the work we have, and the ways in which we manage our lives in general. Here, we also find the reasons why some of us derive great pleasure and satisfaction from life and why others seem to have melancholy thoughts about ourselves and our interactions with others.

Invisible to the naked eye, and, therefore, to our consciousness, these experiences function as guiding factors in our lives until one day in our adult life they surface as reactive behaviours and emotions in our relationship with our partner, the second most intimate relationship after the family nexus in which we spent our childhood. Occasionally, many of our reactions, our behaviour patterns, and the emotions that surface do not seem as if they belong to the person we like to think we are as an adult, and the person we want to be like when we are with our partners.

By using the Dialogue of Acknowledgement, we become more comfortable sharing some of our "old stories" from our baggage with our partners. Doing so can feel threatening and be difficult. The price of not doing it, however difficult it may be, is to run the risk of continuing to behave on the basis of our old values and behavioural patterns, which are making it very difficult to maintain our relationship and the love in our lives. The reward will be new development for us, our partners, and our relationships (Hendrix, 1988).

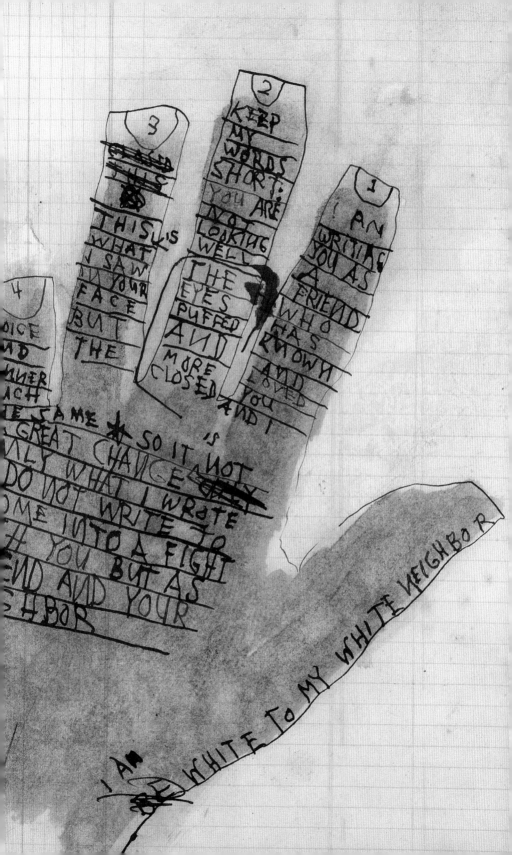

OUR SURVIVAL STRATEGIES GET IN THE WAY

When a child endures a situation where some of his or her most important needs are neglected, the child is forced to develop a series of survival strategies. The strategies are both useful and necessary, and enable the child to get by.

From infancy, the child will attempt to get all its basic needs, such as food, warmth, comfort, and security met by his or her behaviour. Later on, the child's needs become much less obvious and more nuanced. When a child's needs go unnoticed or are rejected, survival strategies start developing. It is necessary for the child to find ways of "being in the world". If a child does not get the understanding, the recognition, and the respect that it so desperately needs, the child is not comforted adequately. He or she may be hungry, or need to suppress aspects that the parents do not like. These reactions are strategies that serve the purpose of adapting to the reality that is the child's life at the time, so that the child either avoids parental anger or wins its parents' love.

When children make frequent use of these survival strategies, they become habits and, thereby, part of the children's and, later, the adults' personality structures. As the child grows older, he or she continues to develop new strategies partly formed by the old ones.

Each of us develops a uniquely personal pattern for tackling the big, difficult, and painful challenges in life. Our survival strategies enable us to deal with the realities of a sometimes cruel and complex world.

However, the problem is that these survival strategies, which we develop as a response to painful and difficult events, will be activated again when we become part of a couple. This is because it is only in our intimate relationships that we encounter criticism and demands with a certain flavour of "sameness", reminding us of our old intimate relational experiences which gave rise to our particular survival strategies.

When, as adults, we use these strategies, we find that not only are they redundant, but they also create new difficulties with our partners. The relevance they represented in childhood no longer obtains; therefore, survival strategies often become the only obstacle to the intimacy and the devotion we seek, creating despair and distance between us. It is as if we start believing that we *are* our survival strategies, although they are just acquired responses that we can change.

The trees that grow on the west coast of Jutland have adapted to the strong west winds by developing their leeside branches only. Our adaptation follows the same pattern. However, unlike trees, we have the opportunity to unfold our branches, when we realize that the winds of the past have stopped blowing. Survival strategies act as a poison to relationship with our partner, because they create insecurity and frustration, and disconnect us from the person we love. What is the matter with her? Why does he suddenly become hysterical or angry, and why do I withdraw in resignation?

When we use survival strategies in our relationships, they instantly become building blocks in the wall between us. As the years go by, the wall seems increasingly insurmountable and impossible to demolish.

Survival strategies can have many faces. Some people become particularly bad-tempered; others lash out verbally or physically. Some bite the bullet and accept the status quo, while others retreat deep into themselves. Some nurse a grievance and become self-pitying; others become hardened inside. Some spin a web of stories, while others turn and walk away. Some take to the bottle, while others get depressed. We hide our sincerity and vulnerability behind our survival strategies.

A certain way to develop a good relationship is to begin to address the problems caused by our survival strategies. In reality, our survival strategies show up in the way we criticize or attack our partner, in our prejudices, in the disconnection between us, and in our disagreements and quarrels.

When we begin to see these behaviours as acquired patterns of response and not as character traits, something new and wonderful will begin to surface in our relationship.

Now

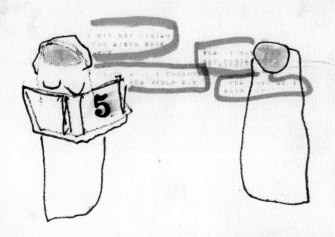

AMSTERDAM W.I.

22   MEI

1970

THE NEW AMSTERDAM SCHOOL
OF ICON PAINTING
(SHIPS) T/O AMSTEL 49 BIJ WATERLOOPLEIN
AMSTERDAM - HOLLAND

THE LOGBOOK
OF THE SHIP
"HENRY DAVID THOREAU"

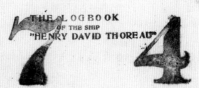

THE ABILITY TO LOVE IS FORMED
DURING INFANCY

I n order to understand what our survival strategies look like and why they have developed as they have, we will take a look at how we as infants formed attachments to other people. The decisive factor in the formation of our survival strategies is the way in which we formed attachments to our mother and/or father or other primary care-givers in those early days. We form what psychologists call either a secure or an insecure attachment.

The ability to form attachments is natural to human beings. Our DNA ensures that a newborn child, from the first day of its life, attempts to contact the surrounding world in order to survive. That explains why, within an hour of being born, infants – regardless of their birth experience – will gaze intensively and calmly at the adults around them. Such eye contact is extremely important and effective in nurturing the bonding and the initial formation of an attachment between the child and its significant others. This innate capacity for attachment continues to develop in the following days.

As early as just a few hours after birth, a child seems able to mimic facial expressions and gestures, such as putting out its tongue or moving an arm with the delay of only a few seconds in response to similar actions by its care-givers. The bonding and attachment process continues, as this makes the adults feel even more that *this child belongs with us.*

Feeling secure is a consequence of the attachment that occurs when the child experiences physical as well as emotional contact, thus feeling understood and protected and safe.

A secure attachment pattern occurs when the child experiences a secure base with parents who build confidence by being there when the child needs them. With this knowledge the child feels secure, begins to explore the world, and experiment with his or her senses and opportunities for play. For this reason, a secure attachment is an essential precondition for the development of our psychological as well as our physical health.

For various reasons, parents may not always be capable of giving their child this good feeling of belonging confidently in the world.

Here the insecure attachment will lead to processes in the child's psyche which have a direct effect on how the child develops its personality and survival strategies, but also on how the child forms other attachments during childhood and as an adult.

We know that a one-year-old child has already developed a pattern of attachment which will have a decisive effect on how it bonds with others in friendship or in love later in life.

INSECURE ATTACHMENT CREATES DIFFICULTIES IN A COUPLE RELATIONSHIP

Our patterns of attachment are crucial because they are essential to a child's development and will show up in a child's natural tendency to do whatever it takes to adapt to the world in which it grows up.

Around 55–60% of us grow up with a secure pattern of attachment. However, the remaining 40–45% will grow up with an insecure pattern of attachment and, in one way or another, experience problems in terms of belonging or attaching to other people later in life.

We will describe three different types of insecure attachment:

- insecure – dismissive, non-committed;
- insecure – anxious, clinging;
- insecure – disorganized, frightened.

The first two patterns of insecure attachment (the dismissive, non-committed and the anxious, clinging), which apply to 40% of us, are common and, thus, are within the range of the "normal", while the last pattern (the disorganized, frightened), which applies to approximately 5% of us, can result in unfortunate scenarios such as a short life expectancy, physical and psychological illness, substance abuse, etc.

Fortunately, parents are not the only people involved in the development of the child's attachment behaviour. There may be an entire hierarchy of other adults who are significant in the child's development. Positive contact we have had with other people inside and outside the family also serves as building blocks for attachment patterns.

Even those of us who have had an extremely tough infancy and childhood have often had some special relations with adults which form the basis of our security and confidence, and the belief in entitlement to life that is necessary to all of us. Children with this experience can be described as "dandelion children", because, in spite of seemingly impossible circumstances in life, they are nevertheless capable of "penetrating the asphalt of life" and blooming.

THE ATTACHMENT BEHAVIOUR OF A PARENT

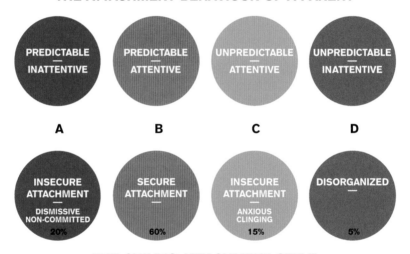

THE CHILD'S ATTACHMENT STYLE

EXPLANATION OF THE GRAPHICS

There is a clear connection between the parents' attachment behaviour and the attachment pattern which the child will develop.

Source: Developed from Seidenfaden and Simon (2003), *Couples Weekend Manual.* Inspired by, and translated from, Harville Hendrix, PhD (1979, revised December 1999) *Getting the Love You Want. Workshop Manual.*

THE ATTACHMENT PATTERN IS REPEATED IN THE COUPLE RELATIONSHIP

Understanding the ways in which our attachment patterns was originally formed is essential because it is this pattern we bring directly into our adult lives and into our couple relationships.

In our baggage we carry an unconscious model of the extent to which we securely and confidently dare to devote ourselves to another human being. This is also a model for the extent to which we have a healthy clear sense of identity, capable of exploring and meeting life's challenges.

For this reason it is extremely useful to look back and get an idea of what kind of "ability to love" we are carrying in our baggage. We need to take a look at whether we have a secure or an insecure attachment pattern and the resulting ways in which we have learnt or adapted to interaction with other people. (See page 72.)

It is important for us to say that we are not talking about pathological states that need treatment. It is possible to lead a completely normal life with insecure attachment patterns. We believe that those of us with insecure attachment patterns will never the less be able to lead lives which fall into the range of "normal". We also believe that it is possible to achieve a secure adult attachment, even if you started out in life with an insecure attachment pattern.

Understanding our lives, reactions, and emotions enables us to liberate ourselves from the limitations of the past and, instead, create new stories about closeness, contact, and vitality.

Knowledge of our attachment patterns is an extremely useful key to the understanding of the way in which we interact with others and the reactions – survival strategies – we use in stressful situations. However, achieving a deeper understanding of our attachment pattern and our identity will, for most of us, require a sharing of formative experiences with our partner or a significant other that will, in turn, allow us to avoid repeating the patterns from our formative childhood years.

We cannot change an unhappy childhood, but sharing reflections on our childhood experiences with our partner or significant other can, in our adult lives, create new understandings. Such insights can be part and parcel of how we change, both separately and together. Sharing, reflecting, and making sense of memories are keys to a happier life for us as adults. So, in a certain sense, it is never too late to have a happy childhood.

For those of us who have had damaging experiences that affect our views on belonging and on being in a relationship, the couple relationship is probably the best point of departure for healing these hurt parts of ourselves.

SECURE ATTACHMENT IN ADULTS

An adult with secure attachment behaviour is able to:

- show and receive love;
- give and receive comfort;
- ask for help;
- form attachments without losing him- or herself;
- experience a "sense of security";
- handle anxiety;
- regulate the body in stressful situations.

Research into adult attachment behaviour has only begun in the last 15–20 years. In our view, this is an extremely important field of knowledge, and we are looking forward to new research results. The research still takes its point of departure in the concepts associated with the formation of attachment during childhood.

ADAPTATION OF THE SELF

There is no single unequivocal psychological model for telling the story of the ways in which we develop our personality. The way we understand development in this book is that growth and development are the direct result of our experiences in our most important relationships. Our first years are decisive in terms of how we learn to live in our relationships and how this learning will impact on our relations for the rest of our lives. This accounts for the many pages focusing on infancy and childhood in our book.

At birth, our brains are not yet developed to process the six basic emotions that later in life characterize us as human beings: anger, happiness, sadness, surprise, dislike, and anxiety. As it develops, our brain gets to know, process, and integrate these emotions into the nuances and depth of experiences of feeling loved or rejected.

An integrated brain is capable of containing the emotions, processing them, and giving them meaning. The brain of a person who nurtures a child can be said to supplement the child's brain, when the child's brain is not yet capable of handling complexity. As a child develops, he or she will show increasingly nuanced ways of relating and being with other people. This capacity will, one hopes, develop and mature throughout the child's life.

The brain that supplements the child's brain needs to be a more integrated brain, a brain that has an empathic understanding of the complexities of a child's perception, and expresses understanding and comfort in a calm, collected, and stable way. The last thing a child needs is that a mother, father, or care-giver becomes overwhelmed by the child's own emotional chaos.

Essentially, it is as if the child's brain is saying, "Help me to control my emotions because I cannot control them myself."

By responding to the child's needs, the mother, father, or care-giver is attempting to match the child emotionally as they interact. It is the quality of this matching that forms the basis of the development of the total emotional, psychological, and physical growth.

EMOTIONAL MATCHING

Early bonding is based on the process of "tuning in to each other's state of mind". The mother and father, or other care-givers, are responsible for establishing and maintaining this link. Recent research indicates that this link is established mainly by the mirror neurons in the uppermost part of the brain.

The nurturing person's first step is to match the child emotionally. This is also described as "listening in", or "seeing", in short, attunement with or matching the child.

In the process of matching, the adult should find his or her own equilibrium, observe the child, and ask him- or herself some basic questions: what is the child preoccupied with at the moment? What do the clues in the body language tell you about the emotional state of the child?

The second step is to relate to the child on the right "emotional frequency". If the child is happy and elated, then the nurturing person responds by entering into this mood and being present in ways that allow him or her to "tune in to" the child's emotional frequency.

MISMATCHING

It is not humanly possible always to match your child emotionally. However, it is essential to be aware of occasions when mismatches occur. Attachment between a child and his or her care-giver must consist of more matching than mismatching episodes. It is also essential that the primary care-givers understand and know how to restore attunement, the emotional matching and harmony, following a mismatch.

Examples of mismatching:

1. An older brother pulls mother's arm while she is nursing his baby sister. He wants mum to play Lego with him. When he

has tried persistently and unsuccessfully to get mother to play, he begins to cry and pulls mother's arm even harder. Now mother gets angry and tells him to stop bothering her, since she is obviously nursing his little sister, and, by the way, he is old enough to play with the Lego himself. He is three years old!

2. A boy is fifteen years old. He no longer thinks that it is a good idea to have fixed agreements about when to visit his father, who lives by himself. Every Wednesday and every other weekend are no longer ideal intervals. He tells his father that he would prefer a more flexible arrangement. The father feels rejected, but does not tell the son. Instead, he says, "Never mind!" Three months go by where they do not talk to each other. Only when the son contacts the father do they meet again.

Emotional matching and the ways in which we meet and understand each other in relationships are central in this book. Our main point is to emphasize that the Dialogue of Acknowledgement can be one of the pathways to a shared emotional matching.

Over and above the attachment behaviour we develop with our parents, other care-givers also contribute to shaping us and our brains. Our care-givers influence us by the way they try to understand and meet us in various scenarios related to our actions and existence in the world.

Research developed during the past 10–15 years gives us reason to believe that attachment in adult life develops according to the same patterns.

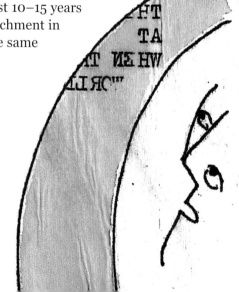

EXERCISE 1

–

WHAT "CHANNELS" ARE YOU BROADCASTING ON?

In order to get a better impression of the parts you are conscious of showing and expressing, as well as the parts you do not express, it will be useful for you to consider what kind of messages you received when you grew up, and how they influenced you within the following four areas of expression.

What was it like:

1) to show emotions in your family? (for example: *Don't be so hysterical!* Or *I sense that you are sad, please tell me about it.*)
2) to develop thoughts? (for example, *Do you have to have an opinion about everything?* Or, *Think about how you want to celebrate your birthday, so we can throw an unforgettable party!*)
3) to take action? (for example, *Do you have to be involved in so many projects at the same time?* Or, *Next time your friend lies, I would suggest that you practise saying no to her suggestions.*)
4) to sense? (for example, *Shouldn't you dress more decently?* Or, *Let's jump in the ocean even if we do not have bathing suits. Nobody will see us!*)

Take some quiet time with each question and let yourself go down memory lane and allow images and thoughts to come to mind. Maybe it is helpful to write down a few notes about how you expressed yourself in your family, together with your parents, your siblings, etc.

Tell your stories while your partner just listens to you.

You can take turns and listen to your partner's stories.

ESTABLISHING BOUNDARIES

The ability to set boundaries for ourselves is, like our ability to sustain closeness, a part of our baggage.

An infant demonstrates his or her needs for boundaries of the self when he or she turns his or her head away after having had eye contact with the mother or the father for a while. If the care-giver insists on maintaining eye contact, the infant will begin to cry, because the need for "recovery" by separation is not being met. The child needs to switch between having and not having contact in order to be in touch with itself.

Setting boundaries is also necessary for us as adults, so that we can develop safe attachments.

With secure attachment patterns, we develop a capacity for connection as well as a capacity for separateness and delimitation. With the "insecure dismissive" attachment pattern, the ability to set boundaries is exaggerated. With the "insecure anxious" attachment pattern, the ability to connect is exaggerated. The child or the adult with a secure attachment pattern will feel secure both when making a connection and when breaking one.

To a child, setting boundaries means that it has more personal space, more time to practise by repeating actions, and more time to develop his or her time for reflection. By setting boundaries safely, the child will also have greater opportunities to obtain and process emotional experiences.

Individuals who have the ability to set their boundaries safely and reflect on their experience will feel integrated into their surrounding world and their relationship network while also having a strong sense of self.

ATTACHMENT THEORY

The concept of attachment came into being in the 1950s. Until that time, it was believed that an infant had only basic needs such as food, sleep and a change of nappies. The prevailing view was also that if a child's needs for food, warmth, and a clean nappy were met, then a healthy development would automatically follow.

However, around 1957, the research of two child psychiatrists, John Bowlby and James Robertson, changed that idea radically. They studied what happened to children who were separated from, and then reunited with, their parents.

Bowlby and Robertson found that even newborn children have an independent drive to actively attach themselves to one or a few people, whether these people give them food or not. In addition, they also saw how significant the consequences are if a child's need to attach to a father, mother, or other care-giver is not met.

Bowlby and Robertson made short films that recorded the behaviour of young children who were hospitalized. At that time, the prevailing view was that parents could only visit their children in hospital once a week. One of these films revolutionized the knowledge about the effect on children of a prolonged separation from parents. *Laura – a Two-Year-Old Child Goes to Hospital* is the title of the short film which follows Laura on a daily basis during a hospitalization that lasted some weeks. The film offers a harsh insight into day-by-day changes in Laura. Originally a happy, curious, and exploring little girl, she becomes more uncomfortable and introverted, and finally just stares impassively into space in a depressed state.

As a result, it became accepted that children react strongly and sustain psychological injuries when separated from their parents or primary carers for prolonged periods of time.

Later in the 1950s, the Canadian psychologist Mary Ainsworth added the concepts of "secure and insecure base" to the theory of attachment. The concept of a secure and an insecure base arises from the fact that all children from infancy need a secure base from which to explore life.

The "secure base" concept developed from the observation that the more secure children are, the less they will cry, the more they will explore, and the more independent they will eventually become. Hence, this was a fundamental revision of the earlier mid-twentieth century view of child development. In those days, the prevailing view was that children who were nurtured too much became too attached to the mother, and that children who were comforted too much became dependent on others.

Today, the ideas of the importance of secure early attachment are well documented and confirmed by recent brain research. Using new brain scanning technology, scientists have observed what happens in the brains of children who grow up with either a secure attachment pattern or with an insecure one. The findings show that in the brains of children with insecure attachment patterns, the area in the brain that, among other functions, performs facial recognition (the orbitofrontal cortex), and the centre which registers time, place, and the degree of awakened basic energy (insula, the temporal lobe) develop many connections to the amygdala, which is the area in the brain that registers danger.

The children with a securely attached pattern show a more evenly integrated brain function.

This can be seen as the brain's way of developing structures and functions to best meet and ensure survival in the game of life. When children cannot trust the people who take care of them, if they do not come when called, or if children are punished when they need comfort, the situation might be perceived as dangerous. The children will then be overcome by fear, which, in turn, is supposed to prompt the "fight, flight, or freeze" response mode. This supports the further development of survival strategies (Holmes, 2001).

DANIEL STERN

The American psychiatrist and psychoanalyst Daniel Stern has, from the mid 1980s onwards, contributed ground-breaking research based on attachment ideas. He has researched the development of infants and the significance of early relation to the development of the self.

Daniel Stern is unique because he does not limit himself to research into the behaviour of children. Instead, he has attempted to understand what is going on in children's minds while they develop.

Using hundreds of video recordings showing the relations between many mothers and children, Stern offers credible and thought-provoking explanations as to how children during their early years begin to experience the shaping of their "self" – Stern calls this "sense of self" – and how their development is influenced by their relationships with their parents.

Stern believes that in order to develop a healthy sense of autonomy as an individual, the child needs to be in a dynamic relationship with his or her environment. Thus, Stern advocates that we, as parents, should aim for relational maturity with our child, rather than aiming to raise an independent child.

Like animals, children will attempt to be close to their mother when they feel threatened. Even when a child has an intense drive to explore his or her own space/world, he or she keeps an eye on mother. Such exploration can only take place at times when the attachment behaviour (the survival strategy) has not been "activated" by something stressful. This means that mother or father represents a reliable refuge, should danger arise. Ideally, it also means that the parents can be protective, calming, and nurturing.

HOW DO WE INTERACT?

The way in which an adult engages with the child and matches, or mismatches it emotionally will have an important effect on the child's learning process with regard to setting his or her boundaries.

Emotional matching is not always positive. This may be due to the parents' conscious attempt to change their child's mood, to quieten or encourage his or her activity or emotional level. Mismatching can be due to the mother's repertoire of states of mind, perhaps misunderstanding the child's emotional state because she is unable to find it in her own experience.

Mismatching resulting from excessive matching may occur when, for instance, a mother over-identifies with her child to the extent that she is constantly hovering over the child, tracking and responding to all the nuances of the child's emotions and maybe even trying to "change", by redefining, how the child feels. In such a situation, it becomes difficult for the child to make a clear distinction between self and other.

Over time, serious consequences may result from different kinds of mismatching, such as the emergence of insecure, or even anti-social, children and adults.

When, as adults, we experience insecurity, we have the same needs as children, that is, emotional (affective) matching with our partner. However, this is where old attachment patterns of rejection or clinging may sabotage the process between us and prevent us from achieving the intimacy and the nurturing we yearn for from our partner. Working with the Dialogue of Acknowledgement is one way for couples to establish such a matching process.

(Stern, 1997)

THE WAY WE TELL OUR STORIES

The way we tell our stories – the narrative aspect – is, to an increasing extent, significant for our ideas about identity and our various approaches to therapy with the philosophies of the postmodern world. It also has an impact on our views about new opportunities and the ways in which we grow in our relationships.

Childhood experiences shape the themes of our lives: the ways we respond, and, thereby, also the form and content of our personal stories. In the story-telling, the teller is associated with the listener, and the story contributes to a shared creation of emotional problem solving between the listening and the telling partners. It is the same principle that is embedded in the Dialogue of Acknowledgement.

Research into attachment has recorded how adults tell stories about their lives (autobiographical stories). What emerges is that the adults with securely or insecurely attached patterns have very different ways of "storying" their childhood.

The stories told by adults representing the four patterns of attachment (see p. 72) can be described as follows:

A: colourless and coherent (insecure, dismissive);
B: colourful and coherent (the securely attached);
C: colourful and incoherent (the insecure, anxious);
D: colourless and incoherent (insecure, disorganized).

We believe that when we engage in the Dialogue of Acknowledgement with our partner, this process contributes significantly to the continued development of our attachment patterns, enhancing the coherence and the colour of the themes in the story about our previous lives.

Stories about ourselves and each other are our minds' attempt to find and make meaning of our rich inner worlds. It is by "storying" that we create or recreate ourselves and our relationships, thereby clarifying differences and consolidating our beliefs and knowledge.

It is for this reason that the development of the self can also be understood as an outcome of the autobiographical process, where new untold stories are added through the processes of the continued storying. Parents may, for instance, help children by developing the story of "And then so and so arrived and . . . and then you said, . . .", etc. In this way, the everyday experiences make sense and contribute to the regulation of a child's state of mind, thereby also enhancing the continued development of the brain.
(Morgan, 2000)

AN EXAMPLE:

During the initial phase of our relationship, Piet would find it upsetting to come home to what he thought was a messy kitchen with dirty dishes. Actually, there were only two dirty teacups. He would complain about that, but to no avail. Working with the Dialogue of Acknowledgement, Piet expressed his considerable frustration and despair at this daily moment of irritation. Using the tools of the dialogue he now remembered all the times when he as a child returned to an empty home, where he had to take charge and was alone without knowing the whereabouts of his parents. Piet became aware of how sad he felt, when he talked about this and that this daily sadness was more or less elicited by the two dirty teacups. The "messy kitchen" invoked old malaise and a sensation of despair and abandonment. The connection between "the two dirty cups" and Piet's melancholy, when confronted with the dirty dishes as a child, became evident, more colourful, and understandable to both of us.

EXERCISES

W e now know that without realizing it, we develop our ability to love based on the influence of our significant others and the culture we grew up in. What we learnt about safety, confidence, care, closeness, respect, and acknowledgement, we carry along into our other relationships in life.

We know that because of our "baggage" we may find reasons to:

- push away the people we love;
- cling to those we love;
- get into conflict with those we love.

It is interesting that, as grown-ups, we have the opportunity to change this process so that our adult love relationships do not continue to unfold with total lack of awareness.

Hence, our task is now to become more at ease with the memories, the influences, and convictions we have about love, closeness, and contact with other people and the origins of these convictions in our childhood.

Find a quiet corner on a peaceful day where you can concentrate on the attachment exercises 2, 3, 4, and 5 without being interrupted. These exercises form important background knowledge for the continued work with the Dialogue of Acknowledgement.

At first, perhaps only a few memories will surface. However, our experience is that when we begin to think about formative experiences, and, even better, when we begin to tell others about them in peace and quiet, then new details and nuances surface.

EXERCISE 2

–

CREATING A PROFILE OF YOUR SIGNIFICANT CARING OTHERS

How to do the exercise:

1. Draw a large pie chart divided into sections that correspond to the number of significant caring others who influenced you in your formative years.

2. Make a list of the characteristics of every single person as you remember them. Use adjectives such as "friendly", "distant", "absent", "warm", "loving", "angry", "cold", etc.

3. If it is difficult to find the right words, you might find inspiration in the list on p. 218.

4. Mark each positive trait with a (+) and each negative trait with a (−).

5. Underline the three most positive traits. Draw a circle around the three most negative traits.

6. Sit down with your partner on a day where you have plenty of time, and tell him or her about what concerns you most. Then it is your partner's turn to tell about his or her preoccupations.

7. Draw on what you have learnt in order to understand some of the frustrations you experience in your everyday life.

Source: Developed from Seidenfaden, K. and Simon, J. (2003), *Couples Weekend Manual*. Inspired by, and translated from, Harville Hendrix, PhD (1979, revised December 1999) *Getting the Love You Want. Workshop Manual*.

EXERCISE 3

–

POSITIVE CHILDHOOD MEMORIES

1. Make a list of concrete positive memories about events that occurred with your significant others such as your mother, father, or other important people in your childhood and adolescence.

2. Emphasize your best memories with each significant other. Draw a circle around the best of these experiences.

3. Now make a new list of your most positive memories with the individual care-givers in childhood and adolescence.

4. If you find it difficult to find the right words, you may find inspiration in the list of character traits on p. 219. Emotions can be described with single words, such as, for instance, "happy", "secure", "loved".

5. Draw a circle around your strongest feelings.

6. Sit down with your partner on a day where you have plenty of time, and tell him or her about what concerns you most. Then it is your partner's turn to tell about his or her preoccupations.

7. Draw on what you have learnt in order to understand some of the frustrations you experience in your everyday life.

Source: Developed from Seidenfaden, K. and Simon, J. (2003), *Couples Weekend Manual*. Inspired by, and translated from, Harville Hendrix, PhD (1979, revised December 1999) *Getting the Love You Want. Workshop Manual.*

EXERCISE 4

–

UNPLEASANT CHILDHOOD MEMORIES

1. Make a list of the negative behavioural traits and painful events which you have experienced with every single care-giver in your youth and adolescence.

2. Underline the most negative experience you have had with every care-giver.

3. Draw a circle around the most negative of the underlined experiences. If you find it difficult to find the right words, you may find inspiration in the list of character traits on pp. 218 and 219.

4. Which negative emotions did you experience with each of the care-givers?

5. Draw a circle around your most unpleasant emotion.

6. What did you fear most about each of your care-givers? For instance, feeling *neglected, shameful, excluded, oppressed, abandoned, despised, outcast, invisible, abused, dominated, suffocated, controlled, ignored.*

7. Draw a circle around your worst fear.

8. What did you long for more than anything from each of your care-givers?

9. Sit down with your partner on a day where you have plenty of time, and tell him or her about what concerns you most. Then it is your partner's turn to tell about his or her preoccupations.

10. Draw on what you have learnt in order to understand some of the frustrations you experience with one another in your everyday life. You might write down your important experiences and concerns in your notebook. Painful memories have a tendency to disappear quickly.

Source: Developed from Seidenfaden, K. and Simon, J. (2003), *Couples Weekend Manual*. Inspired by, and translated from, Harville Hendrix, PhD (1979, revised December 1999) *Getting the Love You Want. Workshop Manual*.

EXERCISE 5

–

WHAT IS YOUR OWN ATTACHMENT BEHAVIOUR LIKE?

1. When you have completed the previous exercises, you will
    begin to develop a clearer idea of your own attachment style
    to your mother and father. The illustration of parental attach-
    ment behaviour on p.72 describes what type of attachment
    behaviour you may develop relative to your parents' attach-
    ment styles. Fortunately 55–60% of all children develop
    secure and good attachment styles (the B type on p. 84).

In terms of the attachment behaviour we develop, we all show
aspects of behaviour from the various attachment styles. Our
predominant attachment behaviour becomes particularly evident
when we feel insecure and experience pressure.

SECURE ATTACHMENT

Secure attachment occurs when the mother is emotionally accessible and supports her child's goal-orientated behaviour. If we, as
children, experience a secure attachment, it seems that we are
capable of reflecting on our own thought processes and dealing
with our emotional experiences, while also demonstrating a
strong and healthy sense of self. We carry these abilities with us
into adulthood.

Secure and confident children are characterized by:

–   being able to give and receive love;
–   being able to give and receive comfort;
–   being able to ask for help;
–   being able to form attachments without fear of losing them-
    selves;
–   having a reliable sense of security.

INSECURE ATTACHMENT BEHAVIOUR

Forty per cent of all children end up with a more or less strained
and fragile ability to form confident attachments – also called

insecure attachment (types A and C). If we have had an insecure attachment as children, we need to constantly monitor and check the parents' physical and emotional availability or, alternatively, withdraw from it. These preoccupations mean that the child loses opportunities for experimenting and creating experiences of his or her own self.

Having insecure attachment behaviour in certain situations should not be considered a life sentence. It is possible to develop secure attachments as an adult.

Adults with insecure attachment behaviour can be divided into two groups, which can be described as follows:

Type A: Dismissive/non-committed (approximately 80% men, 20% women):
– forms attachments with objects, work, projects;
– belittles emotions and does not share emotions and thoughts;
– is prone to self-sufficiency;
– feels malaise in social situations;
– has a tendency to refuse requests for help and prefers working alone;
– has a tendency to withdraw and intellectualize;
– has a tendency to establish rigid rules for self and others in everyday life.

Type C: Anxious/clinging (approximately 20% men, 80% women)
– is often experienced as clinging;
– is excessively conscious of other people's reactions;
– has a tendency to exaggerate own feelings and needs;
– has difficulties with separation;
– has a constant need for contact;
– is prepared to give up own identity in exchange for attachment;
– is excessively generous;
– idealizes the partner and overlooks faults in order to avoid separation and conflict.

Type D: This type constitutes approximately 5%, which have almost exclusively grown up in severely challenged homes characterized by a lack of fundamental care. This segment needs treatment.

INSECURELY ATTACHED PEOPLE OFTEN FIND EACH OTHER

When we look at our own childhood, we see a clear pattern of how each one of us developed our ability to form attachments.

Kirsten remembers:
I grew up in a family where I had a strong attachment to my mother. My father was a diplomat and did not spend much time with the family. He used to say, "Mother takes care of the children and I take care of my career." Because of his career we lived in many different countries. We got used to the fact that attending official functions outside the home was part of the job. Hence, my mother often had to go out and leave us with our nannies. The nannies were often the main figures in our lives.

My mother had a strange habit of never saying goodbye when she left. She could not handle our crying. Hence, I never knew when she was there or not. However, she was attentive and sympathetic when she was with us. My father was predictable and inattentive (he had his work hours and in his private life he had his own interests) and my mother was unpredictable (I never knew when she came and left), but attentive when she was present. As a result, I grew up with an insecure attachment and developed survival strategies by clinging to my mother's skirts – I never knew when she would leave again.

However, I also see an image of myself as a lonely little fighter who has learnt to take care of myself and to please the adults by copying the values they wanted for me – like having a situation under control, being helpful and busy.

All in all this meant that I developed insecure (anxious and clinging) attachment behaviour, where I always arranged things in such ways that I felt I was in control of the contact

I had with other people, thereby feeling a certain sense of security. Hence, I developed difficulties in committing to other people, because I was always unsure of whether or not my partner really wanted me. Later, when I got married, this meant that I had an enormous need to be close and do everything together. If I could have my way, the first thing we would do, when we came home from work would be to sit down and tell each other what we had experienced.

Piet remembers:
I also grew up with an absent father, but on the other hand he was attentive when he was there. From infancy, my attachment to my mother was influenced by her depression. My mother came to Denmark just before the outbreak of the Second World War. Isolated from her family, culture, and language, she was now in an immature marriage and slid into depression. I could not make contact with her and get her to take care of me, nurture me, and give me attention. Hence, I grew up with an unpredictable and attentive father and a mother who was unpredictable and inattentive because she was ill.

Since my father was a liberated, dynamic, and knowledge-able man, I grew up as an argumentative, energetic, and physically active boy. I recall an image of myself smashing all the glass globes on the Christmas tree with a large wooden spoon – with my father's approval. On the other hand, I grew up with a pronounced feeling of not being allowed to be sad and show feelings, because there was nobody to receive and contain them.

The nature of my childhood and adolescence meant that I also developed insecure attachment behaviour (dismissive and non-committed). I kept a distance from other people in order to feel secure and protected. This meant that I could not get my running shoes on fast enough after work. I also had difficulties sharing my feelings, and hence kept many of my sorrows and feelings to myself.

YOUR BRAIN IS A PARTNER
AS WELL AS AN OPPONENT

F ortunately we do not have to be victims of our own story. We all have our baggage, which gives us the opportunity to understand how we communicate and, thereby, also the option of trying to change the way we relate.

As described in the previous chapter, the theories of our survival strategies and attachment behaviour help us to understand our behaviour. In addition, new knowledge about the brain's ways of operating gives us plenty of well-founded hope as to how we can, in fact, change, if we commit ourselves to finding out how we may do so.

The new brain scanning techniques make it possible for us to satisfy our interest in the ways in which the brain develops. These scans show how the various areas of the brain co-operate, and what happens when the brain responds to certain experiences.

The human brain is the most complex biological structure on the planet. Even if our knowledge of the brain is only in the making, we are gradually able to map and understand the brain's amazing working processes. The brain is the major structure in which every experience is stored. Here, everything co-operates in such intricate and complicated networks that it is almost beyond human conception.

The brain is a kind of hard disc, which contains our cumulative memory. A part of this memory is inaccessible to us, but it still influences our reactions and behaviour.

The other part of our memory is accessible via imagination, logic, language, and our ability to put things together. The brain is capable of constant development because of two interesting facts:

- it can be shaped – in medical language this faculty is called neuroplasticity. This means that the brain develops connections between nerve cells, depending on how we use it;
- it constantly develops new brain cells – this faculty is called neurogenesis.

Once we believed that the brain was fully developed by the time it stopped growing, but we now know that was a misconception. While the brain is fully grown at the age of fourteen, it continues to expand and refine its complicated networks between central areas right up until death.

Today, we know that the brain looses a lot of important cells and connections if we do not make use of them or if we do not apply them appropriately: for instance, during stress or other severe types of strain.

On the other hand, we also know that by using all our acquired patterns of reaction, as well as memory and challenges to our intellect, we can transform or improve our brain's ability in many areas. For example, the ability to be an open and wonderful husband or a beautiful and self-assured wife!

The American brain scientist Joseph LeDoux (see p. 111) has described the types of mechanisms at play. His explanations help us to understand what happens when, for instance, we have decided for the umpteenth time not to do a certain thing, and then go ahead and do it anyway, or why we suddenly say the most horrendous things in the heat of an argument, although we know how much they hurt.

His ground-breaking brain research explains how a seemingly banal, peaceful, or insignificant remark or thought expressed by one partner can suddenly spark a completely unmotivated and fierce overreaction in the other partner.

THE LARGE COGWHEEL

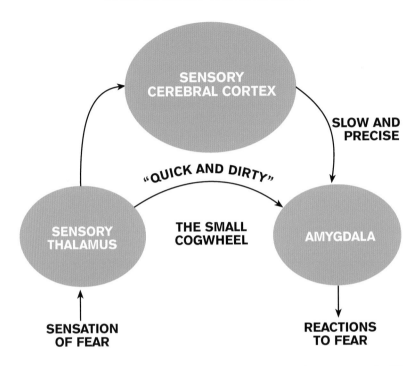

Source: LeDoux, J. (2002). *Synaptic Self – How Our Brains Become Who We Are*. New York: Viking Penguin.

A schematic outline of the pathways of fear in the brain. The fear travels via nerve paths to the sensory thalamus, located at the base of the brain. From there, the fear impulse can either reach "the large cogwheel" (the sensory cerebral cortex) or "the small cogwheel" (amygdala) and eventually produce an emotional response. This is an either/or scenario!

The two pathways differ. In situations characterized by fear, the small cogwheel dominates with its "quick and dirty" reaction. In calm circumstances, the large cogwheel, with its slower and more cogent response, is capable of generating the emotional reaction.

THE PATHWAYS OF AFFECT IN THE RELATION

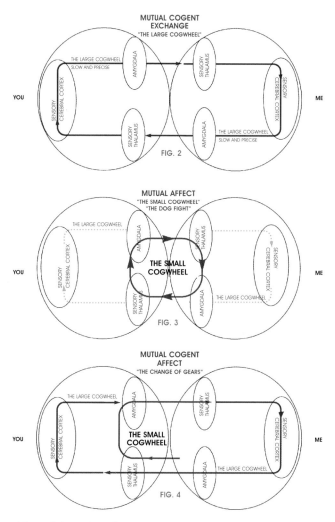

Source: Adapted from Joseph LeDoux.

Figure 2: A couple in an ordinary conversation in the large cogwheel.
Figure 3: The quarrel, the full-blown "dog fight" in the small cogwheel.
Figure 4: The Acknowledging Dialogue, beginning in the small cogwheel and changing gears to the large cogwheel.

THE SMALL AND THE LARGE COGWHEELS

In our therapy with couples it has been quite a revelation to us to find a simple neurobiological explanation as to why we sometimes seek out the lowest common denominator, where we move in the same old groove and wage war on each other although we actually want so many other things.

We call this phenomenon the story of "the small and the large cogwheel". These terms originate from cycling, where the small cogwheel with the small gears are used in steep or difficult terrain, while the large cogwheel and the accompanying gears are used in the large open landscapes without steep gradients.

We use the large and the small cogwheel as symbols of two quite central ways that the brain deals with emotions when we are under pressure, attacked, or exposed. This demonstrates that the nervous system has an "either/or mode" of functioning. It uses either the small or the large cogwheel.

Using the small cogwheel represents the impulsive, reactive, and emotionally charged response. We call it the "quick and dirty" way, because this is where the dog-fights, the major quarrels, the aggression, the territorial marking, the survival strategies, and the fight for reality originate.

The "logic" of the small cogwheel is: *"It is your fault, you stupid bastard . . ., etc.!"*

At this point, we sometimes begin to throw the worst things at each other, verbally and physically. At this stage, we feel caught up in an unavoidable vicious circle, where the reactions are often quite out of proportion to what is happening. Here, we often have a profound feeling of lack of direction and control in our responses when we confront conflicts, anxiety, anger, and despair.

Because of our drive for survival, the human brain is designed to opt for the small cogwheel as a first choice. Nature limits us by our preference for the small cogwheel because our brain, according to Ledoux, in order to protect us in the best possible ways, responds with a "fight, flight, or freeze" reaction when we encounter unsafe situations.

Only milliseconds later, when the affect has subsided, the more productive patterns of reaction may be activated through the large cogwheel.

In short, the small cogwheel is the part of the nervous system that ensures survival. But it comes at a price! The price we pay is that occasionally we behave like brain amputees – because there is no connection to the large cogwheel's higher brain functions (see below). In this situation, we hurt, degrade, and treat our partners in undignified ways.

The large cogwheel represents a slower mode of response. It is characterized by reflection and afterthought, and it draws on parts of our memory, experience, sense of humour, creativity, knowledge, language, faculties of thought, and combining abilities.

The large cogwheel allows us to contain other people, to listen and not just jump to the nearest conclusions and interpretations. The large cogwheel is the point of origin of everything that constitutes the person's make-up, and this is also where he or she can develop the ability to concentrate and be present.

The logic of the large cogwheel is: *It makes sense that you . . . when you experience . . .*", etc.

THE GEAR AND THE CHANGE OF GEARS

Of course, the goal is not just to learn how to manoeuvre with the large cogwheel. We need both cogwheels. Without the small cog-wheel there would be no focus, because the small cogwheel is the point of entry to the old stories, the "this reminds me of" stories, which are the foundation of new growth and development.

The major challenge is that some of us operate too much with the small cogwheel in our close relationships without knowing why or how to change gears, or how to co-operate with our partner to integrate the functions of the large, constructive, and thoughtful cogwheel.

Mastering the change of gears between the large and the small cogwheels is the central subject of this book, because it is the way to effect change and create new ways of being together.

SUMMA SUMMARUM

When one partner is steaming with fury, there is an urgent need for the other partner to contain, acknowledge, and be patient, so that the angry partner can gradually catch up with his or her "entire person" (the melting point), because it is only a small part of the person that is impelling them to want to throw cups and plates.

These "small cogwheel situations" are the ultimate tests of The Acknowledging Dialogue. If it succeeds, we experience how we can avoid participating in a dog-fight (again). Instead, we create a secure space, where acknowledgement, empathy, and reflection have the upper hand.

When we encounter difficulties in our relationships, we have a choice. We do not have to resort to going on autopilot – reacting with the small cogwheel. We may either continue to perceive our partner as the cause of our mad circuit on the small cogwheel, or we might, as partners, see ourselves and each other as people who create the preconditions for a change of gear into the large cogwheel.

The change of gear from the small to the large cogwheel is an amazing experience. Even if it seems as if we just want to shout and throw cups and plates, it is possible to find rhyme and reason in the "madness" together and, thereby, stop the dog-fights.

First, the story is acknowledged by the partner, and then it begins to make sense to the person who was operating from the small cogwheel. This person will feel contained and supported and will then be able to continue in the large cogwheel with his or her partner.

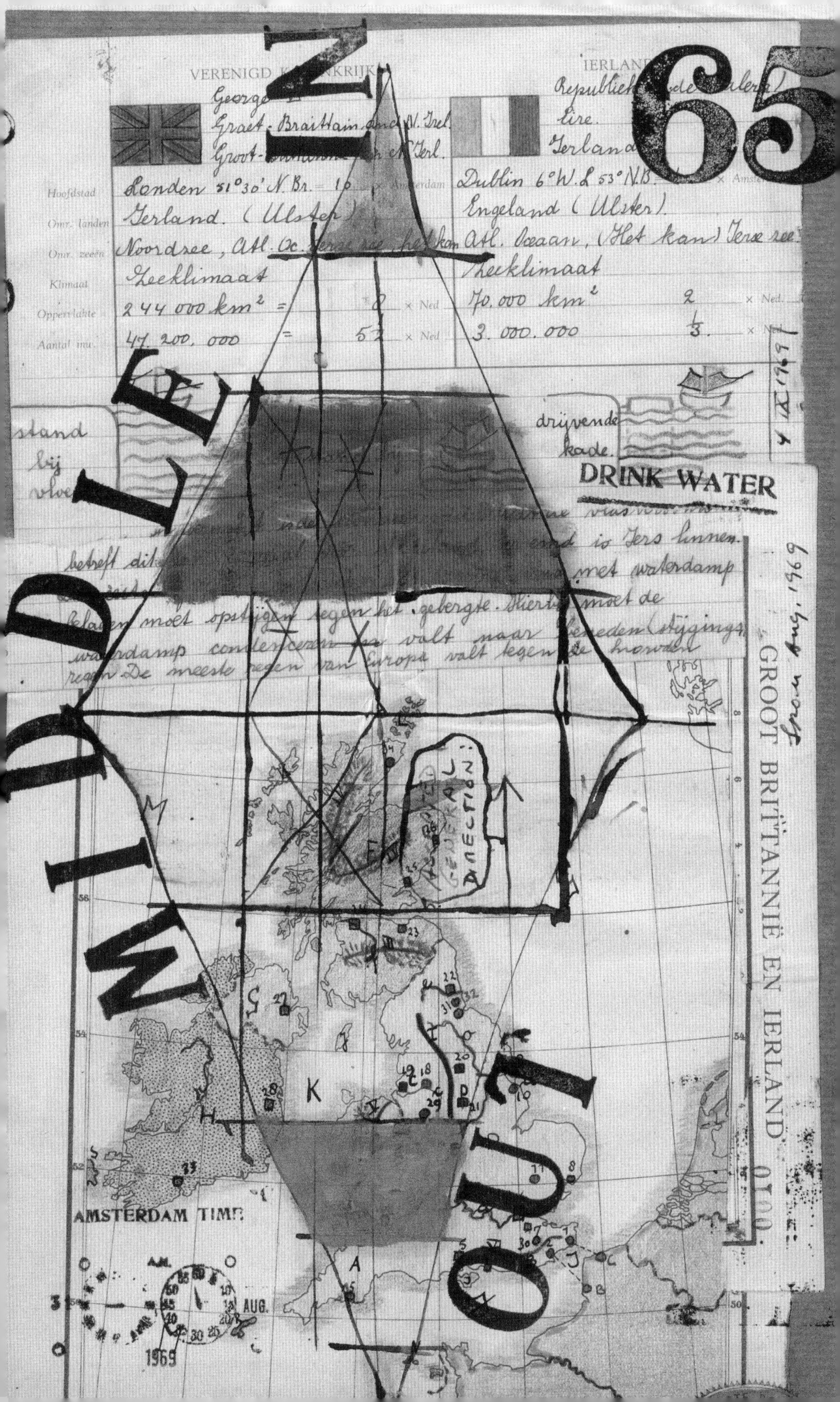
65
N
VERENIGD
IERLAND
Great-Brittain and N. Irel.
Eire
Hoofdstad
Londen 51°30' N.Br.
Dublin 6° W.L. 53° N.B.
Omr. landen
Ierland (Ulster)
Engeland (Ulster)
Omr. zeeën
Noordsee, Atl. Oc.
Atl. Oceaan, (Het kan) Ierse zee
Klimaat
Zeeklimaat
Oppervlakte
244 000 km²
70.000 km²
Aantal inw.
47.200.000
3.000.000
drijvende kade
DRINK WATER
GROOT BRITTANNIË EN IERLAND
AMSTERDAM TIME
A.M.
AUG.
1969

THE CHANGE OF GEARS

Lisbeth and Lars are in the middle of a major renovation of their house. It is far from completed. One day, on the way home in the car, Lisbeth says that she has seen some nice, inexpensive bookshelves, which would fit nicely into the new living room. She asks, *"Couldn't we go and buy them now?"*

Lars responds with the suggestion that they postpone buying the bookshelves until they have a place to put them. Right now garages and cellars are bursting.

Lisbeth feels rejected, and, full of despair, she says, *"I am at the point of giving up on that house."*

Lars reacts drastically by "freaking out". Finally, he shouts, *"Do not put any more pressure on me . . ."* (He is on the small cogwheel.)

Lisbeth suggests that they pull over. They sit quietly for some time and the tears are rolling down Lisbeth's cheeks. Lars feels unfairly criticized and says in a loud voice, *"You pressure me. There is nothing more I can do. The architects have let us down, the builders do not turn up, and the building authorities obstruct our plans. I feel completely stuck and there is no way I can deal with having to spend money on furniture now – furniture which, by the way, we have nowhere to put."*

Lisbeth is still frightened and silent. (She is struggling with her own sense of injustice in order to remain in the large cogwheel.) After some quiet time, she says, *"I actually understand that you freak out when you feel pressured by all these issues."*

Lars continues to talk in a quiet voice about his worries. The temperature rises in the car. Lars feels more at ease now that he has told his story and it has been acknowledged by Lisbeth. He is also just about ready to face his own strong reaction. In short, he is ready to change gears and move on to the large cogwheel, where they can discuss what happened. This means that Lisbeth will also get the chance to unfold her story. His anger frightened her, but she also needs to talk about the frustrations involved in living with three children in her aunt and uncle's house. Furthermore, she wants to use the stage of waiting to find the right furniture at a sensible price.

In the process where both tell their story in "the large cogwheel", Lars realizes that it reminds him of how his father often criticized him as a child and how Lars had the experience that he never performed well enough. Lisbeth realizes that she, as a child, often experienced that her mother restricted her, and that she had to submit to her mother's wishes and demands. Lisbeth now experiences Lars' anger in a new way and Lars acknowledges Lisbeth's frustration.

Lisbeth and Lars

Neurobiology helps us understand why we constantly get into fights with those near and dear to us. Fortunately, it also tells us that it is possible to work with the brain in the same ways that we train our body – with similar amazing results.

By becoming aware of our brains' patterns of automatic responses, we can find a greater balance between our affect and impulses and our ability to reflect and contain. This means that we can learn to protect ourselves from stress because we focus on developing ways of reducing our primitive reactions and our readiness to fight. Instead, we want to enhance all the wonderful and marvellous abilities we have as human beings.

Research tells us that whether we are operating with the small or the large cogwheels, we have choices. Our brains are designed in such a way that we are able to develop a capacity to control our temper and emotional responses. We can start this process if we use our understanding to train aspects of our brain which are not particularly well developed.

So, yes, we can change!

Brain research gives us a lot of hope and opportunities for change that we perhaps have not been aware of. The Dialogue of Acknowledgement gives us the opportunity of change. That is, if we are motivated! Love at its best.

When Per Returned

Per had begun working in a new job. It was extremely challenging and he was obviously exhausted. As the weeks went by, the "old Per" returned. He performs excellently with the small cogwheel. This image had struck both of us like a bolt of lightning when we learnt about the Dialogue of Acknowledgement and the brain's response to "the large and the small cogwheel".

I sensed it first, and then our daughter began to notice.

Per was "quick and dirty", snappish, insensitive, and rigid, and seemed to have lost his otherwise marvellous ability to see and hear me as well as our daughter. We had almost begun to take his wonderful ability for granted. At first, I tried to tell him how I experienced the change. Nothing happened except resistance and counter-attack. Then I was sad, withdrew and sulked a little, but to no avail. The chain actually only jumped off the small cogwheel, when our daughter, after her confirmation, said to him, "It is as if I am not here, if I were gone, you would not notice. You never want to play, and just keep telling me to wait a minute."

Then something dawned on Per. An opportunity occurred that meant that we could begin to talk about it. He now realized that he was unhappy about his insensitive behaviour and gradually he began to be able to see and hear himself again. The change from the large to the small cogwheel had only taken a couple of weeks, but long enough for me to become frightened and insecure again. I did not feel very well at the confirmation, I had said. At large family gatherings I need fundamentally to be strong. I am strong, when Per and I are on good terms and have a good and secure mutual connection; where I, metaphorically speaking, feel his hand around my waist. However, on the day of the confirmation, he was not there for me. He did not notice me, and appeared not to notice that I needed him. This scenario reawakens all my memories of unresolved emotions in my baggage.

For this reason we were both incredibly relieved to find out that it was possible for us to get back on the right track again quite quickly. On this track – the large cogwheel – problems are solved and hurts are healed. The most amazing thing was that Per, almost from one day to the next, was able to change gears from the small to the large cogwheel – apparently just by deciding to do so. He accessed a pattern of behaviour embedded in the "hard disc" of his brain that had been unavailable. It was indeed really scary that that was all it took.

I grew to respect him so much more for his willingness to make this change. In fact, I was very touched.

Mette

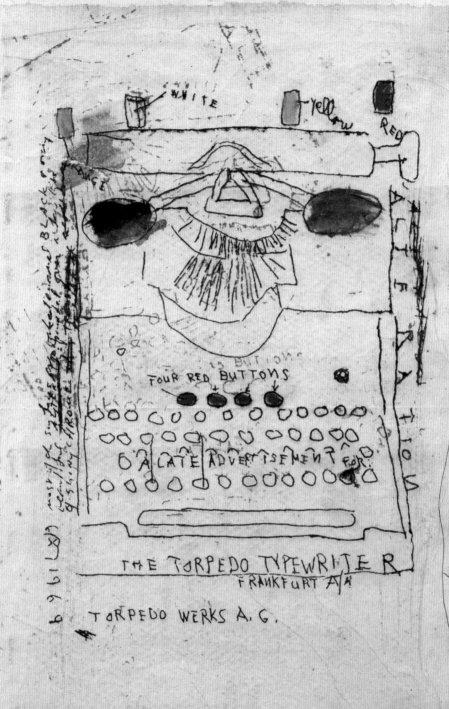

WHITE   yellow   RED

FOUR RED BUTTONS

A LATE ADVERTISEMENT FOR

THE TORPEDO TYPEWRITER
FRANKFURT A/M

TORPEDO WERKS A. G.

THE PATHWAYS OF FEAR ACCORDING TO JOSEPH LEDOUX

The American professor Joseph LeDoux specializes in brain research. For the past twenty years he has investigated how emotions and affect, particularly fear, are produced and processed in the human brain. He was trained as a computer scientist, but branched into the enormous, largely uncharted territory of how emotions are generated in the brain.

Anxiety is also a function of the brain's fear system, which is located in two almond-shaped groups of neurons known as the amygdala, situated in the deep layers of the brain. In this area of the brain you find the memory, the emotions, and their mutual connections.

LeDoux's research has contributed to the debate on what constitutes our humanity. The concerns and the criticism of this debate are focused on whether or not the human personality can now be reduced to connections between nerve endings (LeDoux, 2002).

MENTALIZATION ACCORDING TO PETER FONAGY

Peter Fonagy is a British psychoanalyst and scientist who is excellent at communicating his research. He has succeeded in integrating attachment theory, developmental theory, and new neurobiological knowledge in the treatment of borderline patients.

Mentalization is our ability to sense and form realistic beliefs about other human beings' states of mind. Normally, this ability is mastered in social exchanges: for example, in a well-functioning interaction between mother and child, between lovers, or among friends.

The concept of mentalization could possibly be considered as one of the most important building blocks in our way of understanding interaction with each other. This concept explains our ability as human beings to influence each other in intricate ways (Fonagy, 2002).

So, in a sense, our ability to mentalize might be lacking in the large and small "survival episodes" – the relationship conflicts – shown in Figures 2 and 3.

The growth in a relationship might also be described as an expansion in the capacity for mentalization, even if it does not sound very poetic. The Dialogue of Acknowledgement is one of the pathways to facilitate this expansion.

Neurobiology is an important element to keep in mind when considering the larger perspective of the challenging art of maintaining a satisfying relationship with a partner. The reason is that when we have a better understanding of the brain's reactions, we are able to act in more goal orientated and balanced ways, instead of resorting to the demanding, destructive, and immediate "fight or flight reactions" through the small cogwheel.

According to Peter Fonagy, increasing mentalization ability will have clear and dramatic consequences for psychotherapy in terms of supporting the development of:

- satisfying interpersonal relations (what happens between two people);

- the ability to reflect while experiencing strong emotions, as opposed to joining in the dog-fight;

- the capacity to identify the impact on oneself as opposed to reacting to the affect with the small cogwheel.

These processes all represent an expanded mentalization capacity.

THE MIRROR NEURONS

We are only now beginning to understand the mechanisms of empathy and sympathy. The ability to put ourselves in other people's shoes is one of our most important human abilities. The mirror neurons in our brains may be a decisive element in this ability.

Experiments with monkeys show that not only do they respond to actions, they also seem able to sense the intention behind an action. In a manner of speaking, they are able to imagine the thinking behind an action. It was a coincidence that drew the scientists' attention to this central function of the mirror neurons. One of the scientists shook a bag of peanuts and began to eat them. The cages housing the monkeys with brain electrodes attached were within hearing range, but the monkeys could not see the scientist. The scientist noticed that the monitors showed that this sound activated the brain centres that would also have been activated if the monkeys had been eating peanuts themselves. Thus, much more than the hearing centre in the brain was activated by the sound of the peanuts in the bag. This discovery led to fruitful research in which the function of the mirror neurons were indentified and described.

There is a close relationship between actions and emotions – we automatically interpret the emotional meaning of movements. In this way, we seem to have taken the first minor step towards gaining knowledge of the mechanics of understanding other people's emotions and empathic knowledge.

Anxiety, tension, or stress reduces the function of the mirror neurons significantly. This means that our capacity for empathy is limited, which again explains the well-known phenomenon that when we are highly stressed and feeling intense emotions, we behave as if we were brain amputees.

The language centre of the brain is located near the mirror neurons. This means that listening to another person's story also activates the mirror neurons. Mirror neuron processes are a prerequisite of being able to be in relationships with other people. We can understand the mirror neuron system as a system facilitating social orientation (Hart, 2006).

SEXUALITY:
A FORM OF ELECTRICITY

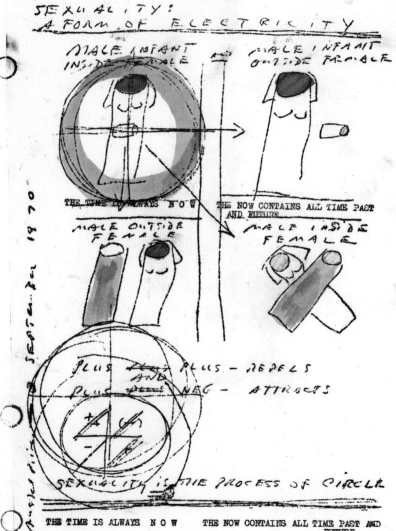

MALE INFANT
INSIDE FEMALE

MALE INFANT
OUTSIDE FEMALE

THE TIME IS ALWAYS NOW   THE NOW CONTAINS ALL TIME PAST
AND FUTURE

MALE OUTSIDE
FEMALE

MALE INSIDE
FEMALE

PLUS AND PLUS - REPELS
PLUS AND NEG - ATTRACTS

SEXUALITY IS THE PROCESS OF CIRCLE

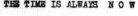

THE TIME IS ALWAYS NOW   THE NOW CONTAINS ALL TIME PAST AND
FUTURE

Amsterdam September 1970

HOW ABOUT TONIGHT, DARLING?

A joyful sexuality can be the place where the relationship is experienced most intensely, where children are conceived and where we generate new energy, new courage, and an intense shared life. Sexuality can be the glue that sustains the relationship. Being sexual is a dialogue, which may be non-verbal, which works. There is devotion, playfulness, experimentation with roles, etc.

When it works, then there is no need to talk about sexuality. *"If it ain't broke why fix it?"*

But what if the question, "How about tonight, darling?", feels invasive and causes you to break out in a sweat? You feel like saying, "No, not tonight," or you attempt to withdraw in less obvious ways.

What if the differences between you, which used to turn you on, have changed so the fire now burns lower?

When something is unsatisfactory and does not work, we may need to open up to one another. The Dialogue of Acknowledgement is an excellent, supportive, and kind way of opening up a topic that may never before have been articulated or explored. There might be shame or guilt, as well as great differences involved. It is difficult to talk about, more difficult to act upon, and it becomes even more complex if we ignore it.

We often find that an unsatisfactory sex life can be the decisive factor that prompts a couple to opt for therapy. This is a very good decision, because often it is not just the sexual relationship that has died. If there is no vigour and vitality in the relationship in general, then the erotic and sensual aspects also tend to suffer.

Let us just establish here and now that it is quite natural that erotic desire comes and goes for longer or shorter periods during a lifetime. Pregnancy makes some women feel uncomfortable when having sex, and many parents with small children may feel that their desire to have sex is suddenly not as great. They are quite simply too tired, and give so much of themselves to the children that there is no energy left for sex.

A lack of desire to have sex can also occur if we are preoccupied with something else for a period of time, so that we do not think much about our sexual needs. In addition, if we do not talk about this, it may become a problem.

In some relationships a polarization might also occur with the effect that the woman never feels desire for sex, while the man always feels like having sex. For others, the sexual aspect of their relationship comes to a grinding halt because one of the partners has lost respect for the other, or one has been unfaithful.

In addition, in our culture, we live with a huge emphasis on sexual gratification, which puts our sexual drive under unreasonable pressure. It is difficult not to be affected by the fantasy ideal of a wrinkle-free, inventive, and fit sex partner, who is also a focused parent with a demanding career.

Desire, sensuality, and erotic appetite should not be taken for granted. We are not turned on by each other automatically, especially if we have lived together for many years. It is like love. Every so often, we must invest in our sex life with special energy and attention in order to find new freedom and pleasure.

A lack of desire can often become a vicious circle. When our partner makes advances, we hold back and avoid nudity so as not to arouse her, or don't wear the low-necked blouse in order not to arouse him. In these ways, we move still further away from the intimacy that could revive the passion.

THE REAL VOYAGE OF DISCOVERY CONSISTS NOT IN SEEKING NEW LANDSCAPES, BUT IN HAVING NEW EYES

– MARCEL PROUST –

A HORMONAL EXPLANATION

Women as well as men produce the hormone testosterone, one of the many factors which influences desire and sex. Thus, a low sex drive might be due to a low testosterone level – also called low T.

It may be liberating and reassuring to both parties in a relationship to remember that the foundation of sexual energy is multifaceted. Depending on our survival strategy, we might reason quickly: "Oh, there is probably something wrong with me." Or: "Maybe there is something wrong with you!" Both responses are counterproductive.

In Denmark, there is no general access to either measurement of testosterone or treatment of low T. It turns out there are many side effects and risks involved in hormonal treatment (for instance, the development of secondary male characteristics in women and prostate cancer in men). For good reasons, the health authorities have chosen a cautious approach.

Regardless of whether or not there are medical–biological explanations, it is crucial to view differences in, and difficulties with, sexual desire as a shared concern.

Hence, we would like to point to our dialogical processes as pathways towards clarification, understanding, and recognition of the differences in this area as well as in all other areas of your relationship.

Once we are able to share the preoccupations and thoughts we may have, things settle down and then the shame and the guilt will disappear. Shame and guilt occur naturally, when we back out or resign impulsively – or do whatever our survival strategy dictates.

Using the Dialogue of Acknowledgement, you have the best basis for containing and motivating each other to participate in a sexual relationship in ways that feel good for you both (Love, 2001).

SHAME IS MEN'S GREAT SEX KILLER

In her book, *Hot Monogamy*, Pat Love, who is a psychologist in Austin, Texas, describes a number of new and surprising aspects about sexual relationships. She interviewed 1500 couples and discovered, among other things, that shame destroys men's sexual desire. In addition, Pat Love found a great number of ways in which women shame their men:

- most women do not understand how much joy a man gets from pleasing a woman. Especially not how much it means to the man to please the woman he lives with;

- it is easy for women to show how frightening men can be to women because of their physical strength, but women are unaware of their own strength in terms of shaming;

- many women do not realize the extent to which they criticize or make demands on their men. When they are confronted with their critical approach, their most common reaction is: "But I am only trying to make him a better person.";

- what women often perceive as their partner's withdrawal and lack of interest is often a sign that their partner is overwhelmed by criticism and a feeling of despair.

Examples of women shaming:

- when a woman excludes the man from important decisions: "*I have made an agreement with the children that . . .*";

- when a woman deprives him of the opportunity to help: "*Don't worry about that, I will take care of it.*";

- when a woman corrects him in the company of others;

- when a woman makes unrealistic demands on his time;

- when a woman focuses on what you did not get as opposed to what you received;

- when a woman talks in a hard reproachful tone of voice;

- when a woman questions his work: *"What have you actually been doing all day?"*;

- when a woman criticizes his family;

- when a woman interprets his statements: *"What you really meant, when you said you were tired, was that you do not feel like listening to me."*;

- when a woman generalizes: *"You always criticize me."*

WOMEN OFTEN FEEL ABANDONED

On the other hand, Pat Love also discovered that the worst thing a man can do to a woman's sexual drive and feelings for the relationship is to leave her alone in the marriage. Unbeknown to the man, a woman may feel abandoned on many different levels. For instance, when men are unable to be present emotionally.

Examples of men's abandoning behaviour:

- when he is not involved in her or does not see her. When he does not listen to her dreams;

- if both are tired when coming home from work and he withdraws in order to unwind;

- she may feel that they can meet erotically and sexually, but subsequently she might miss the closeness;

- if he does not involve her in his depressions. His way of overcoming sadness or a menacing depression might be to keep it to himself, while she wants to share the feelings;

- she might feel abandoned because she fears his anger. The great majority of men are not aware of how frightening and terrorizing their anger seems and how it prevents her from reaching out to him.

The ways in which we mediate these thoughts to each other are, however, crucial. If we confront our partner with the statements above in blaming ways, then we are back to square one.

The secret is that by changing our behaviour, we pave the way for our partner's desire to change his or her behaviour. Women will have more loving and caring partners if they acknowledge men's vulnerability to shame and reduce the kind of behaviour that elicits shame in men. Men will experience that women can be more in touch with their sexuality if men do not create a sense of abandonment, and acknowledge that women's sexuality is focused on closeness, intimacy, and openness.

DO NOT FORGET THAT THOSE
WHO LOVE YOU THE MOST
ARE THE PEOPLE
YOU CAN HURT THE MOST

– RICHARD C. MILLER –

DESIRE AND SELF-ESTEEM ARE CLOSELY RELATED

Henrik and Anne are two years into their relationship. Anne has brought three young girls into the union. Anne is an ambitious, hardworking schoolteacher and a politically active mother. Henrik is a big strong teacher who works with maladjusted children. Both have many challenges in their lives – keeping the family together in practical and financial ways – so there is not a lot of surplus energy and time for each other.

They are still very fond of each other. However, when they spend time alone, Anne experiences that Henrik does not really have desire for her. On the other hand, Henrik feels under pressure and thinks that he cannot live up to what he imagines are Anne's sexual longings.

When Anne stops criticizing him and begins to listen more to him, he is able to tell her how much he likes her, and how afraid he is of losing her. Henrik is ready to be there for her and her children 100%, but essentially he is afraid of not being good enough.

In becoming aware of the effect criticism has on him, he taps into the atmosphere in his childhood home. In particular, Henrik remembers his relationship with his father and his father's constant demands, criticism, and shaming. Henrik felt that he was never able to do anything well enough.

Henrik realizes that he harbours a longing for his father's appreciation and acknowledgement of all the things he has actually done for his parents. His fear of feeling shamed now surfaces when his wife criticizes and blames him, and when he wants to show his erotic devotion and vulnerability.

Anne and Henrik

EXERCISES

The following exercises may be seen as suggestions and opportunities that can help you increase your knowledge of each other in general. They might also be useful approaches when you have difficulties with intimacy.

EXERCISE 6

–

MY THOUGHTS ABOUT OUR SEXUALITY

Each of you takes time out to prepare yourself for a dialogue.

1. Consider the following:

    – what I would like my partner to do when we are sexually intimate, is to . . .

    – one way in which I make it difficult for him or her to give me what I want is to . . .

    – one way in which I could make it easier for my partner to give me what I want is to . . .

    – in terms of my partner's sexual needs, I am aware of . . .

2. Each of you takes turns of approximately twenty minutes where you tell your partner about issues that concern you. One person tells while the other person listens. There should be no questions. Silence is quite OK. Do not interrupt the silence. Silence sparks off new thoughts.

3. Conclude the exercise with the words: "Thank you for sharing this with me."

EXERCISE 7

–

MORE THOUGHTS ABOUT OUR SEXUALITY

1. Consider the following questions:

    –   how many times a day/week do you feel sexually aroused?

    –   what is it like for you, when we have not had sex for several days/weeks?

    –   what part does sex play in your life?

    –   are there any particular times, when you feel sexual desire?

    –   what do you feel when I am not interested in making love?

    –   what is it like for you when I am interested in having sex and you are not?

    –   what is it like for you when we make love and you are not initially interested?

    –   what is it like for you when you have to suppress your sexual needs because I am not turned on?

    –   when do you feel most excited sexually?

2. Each of you takes turns to talk for twenty minutes about issues that concern you. One person speaks while the other listens. There should be no questions at this stage. Silence is quite OK. Do not break the silence – it may generate new thoughts.

3. Conclude the exercise with the words: "Thank you for sharing this with me."

SOME TIPS FOR BETTER SEX

- You yourself have a part to play in creating the environment and getting in the mood for sex.

- Make the time – and take care not to be too tired.

- Accept that you and your partner have different levels of desire. One of the characteristics of happy couples is that they view sexuality as an opportunity for intimacy and that they do not perceive differences in needs and wishes as personal criticisms. Bear in mind that a person with low desire feels less inclined to have sex once the first love and infatuation have passed and the children have arrived. It is, however, possible for a person with a low level of desire to be an incredible sex partner if he or she is inspired by the wish to give and receive pleasure. However, this requires that the partner who has a strong sex drive is capable of accepting that the person with the low sex drive is motivated by love and devotion to the relationship, and not necessarily by physical needs or sexual desire. In this situation, it is also necessary that the person who has a strong sex drive understands that for the person with low desire it involves a great effort and concentration to get turned on and into the right mood. Hence, the person who has a strong sexual drive should also be involved in the motivation of his or her partner – perhaps on completely different levels.

- Be willing to receive sex as a gift. If neither of the partners in the couple is interested in sex, then there may not be a problem, but if only one partner wants sex, then it can be a challenge for both partners. Quite a number of couples show up in the consultation room with a more or less open contract that often sounds like: "I expect you to be faithful to me, but you should not expect me to meet your sexual needs." What can we do if one of the partners wants sex and the other does not? The fundamental issue is that we should do what is best for the relationship!

PART
2

THERE
IS THE LIVING
FLOWER
WHICH DIES
& THE DEAD
FLOWER
WHICH
LIVES.
THERE
ARE
BOTH

PATHWAYS TO THE
VIBRANT RELATIONSHIP

Welcome to Part II, which focuses on concrete and practical ways to engage with the Dialogue of Acknowledgement. In this dialogue, we use frustrations and criticisms in the relationship to create new confidence, connection, and empathy.

Frustration and criticism are the golden elements in our everyday life, which we will use to recreate the magic and the wonderful openness and understanding we felt way back then, when we loved each other body, mind, and soul.

The Dialogue of Acknowledgement is a reciprocal process, which enables us to dissolve the Gordian knot that occasionally develops in love relationships, when the power struggle proves insurmountable. This process will help to loosen the knot and provide the couple with sufficient insight and empathy to "unravel the threads".

From this point onwards, the pathway is cleared for the vibrant relationship, characterized by mutual closeness, genuine intimacy, and shared thoughts about what is important to love and a shared life.

The central axes of the continued work are:

- maintaining closeness and contact;
- communication that is acknowledging and communication that is non-acknowledging;
- appreciative communication;
- dialogue.

MAINTAINING CLOSENESS AND CONTACT

Closeness is just as significant a precondition for the well-being of human beings as food, water, and oxygen. That is the way we are made! Closeness is a necessary condition for our development.

This was first demonstrated during the Second World War, when the psychoanalyst René Spitz studied children who had been sent to orphanages. Here, he monitored children who were given only food, had sufficient sleep, and were kept clean. Death rates among these children were very high.

Moreover, children in various social environments were monitored when closeness and contact were added to the general care. René Spitz found that closeness and contact were decisive factors in their well-being and survival. It was proved beyond any doubt that closeness and contact were essential for children to thrive, much more so than peace, quiet, and cleanliness.

Human beings are formed and influenced in decisive ways by the close relationships they experience while growing up and later seek in adult life. As we described with the attachment styles (see p. 70), it is through interacting with others that the capacity to be present, attentive, and grounded is formed. The ability to establish and maintain intimacy with others and maintain it cannot be taken for granted. It is an ability that has its roots in our childhood experiences.

Hence, there is good reason to assume that the closeness that is vital to children is also essential to the well-being and development of adults. Closeness and contact are the indispensable prerequisites for growth in adult relationships.

CONFIDENCE GENERATES CLOSENESS

When we seek a close and intimate relationship, the longing for closeness is the driving force. We look for someone to share our thoughts, emotions, and lives with, someone who understands and likes everything about us. It is in the close association with others that we experience our selves most intensely.

Closeness in the relationship occurs when we find a "safe harbour" with each other; when we not only hear each other, but have the ability to listen to what our partner has to say. This means taking in what our partner says and gradually digesting it. Closeness is also caring – seeing our partner with new eyes uncontaminated by criticism and old prejudices. However, even if we desire closeness more than anything else, in many relationships we create the exact opposite: unrest, distance, quarrels, loneliness, or emptiness.

As described in Part I, there are many good reasons for these things happening. Insecure attachment styles, strong inappropriate survival strategies, and too much brain activity on the "small cogwheel" are possible explanations. The direct road to greater closeness lies in becoming aware of the mechanisms in ourselves and our partners that prompt us to cut ourselves off from the source of closeness.

ACKNOWLEDGING AND NON-ACKNOWLEDGING COMMUNICATION

It is important to understand the full meaning of the word acknowledgement. When we acknowledge something our partner has told us, we relate to our partner's reality. The result is that our partner feels both seen and heard. We acknowledge the logic in the story and that we have understood the story. However, this does not necessarily mean that we agree with what has been said.

To show acknowledging behaviour means that:

- we take it for granted that there are several ways to understand reality;
- for a time, we have the ability to see the world from someone else's perspective;
- we do not have all the answers as to why the relationship is as it is.

It follows that:

- acknowledgement is not the same as praise;
- acknowledgement does not mean that we do or should agree;
- acknowledgement also involves dealing with negativity.

An example of an acknowledging conversation would be:

Your partner is extremely angry because you came home late.

"I understand that you are angry. I should have called and informed you, so that you could have planned accordingly."

If you already called home and informed your partner about the delay, an acknowledging conversation could begin like this:

"I see that you are very angry that I have come home late, even though I called and told you so. Please help me understand why you are so angry!"

The search for a deeper understanding beyond the anger continues until, we hope, it becomes possible for you to come to a genuine acknowledgement/understanding of your partner's anger.

IT IS EASIER FOR US TO BE CRITICAL

Unfortunately, there are many factors operating against the use of acknowledging language. In our ways of communicating with each other we include the use of many critically charged expressions about what is not working, while also focusing on what we do not understand or what we disagree about. Criticism comes more easily than expressing what we yearn for or focusing on what works and inspires us in our relationship.

You can return to the acknowledging communication by:

- applying positive words instead of criticizing;
- focusing on positive messages and not on the critical statements;
- focusing on the strengths instead of the faults.

CHARACTERISTICS OF NON-ACKNOWLEDGING COMMUNICATION:

- "But" is a problematic word in an acknowledging conversation.
  "I understand what you are saying, but . . ."

As soon as you use a "but", it cancels the significance of your previous statement. You are no longer fully present in your partner's reality. You have retreated into your own world.

- Interpretations create distance and are breeding grounds for feeling misunderstood.

"*When you close the door in that way, I know that you are angry with me.*" The interpretation is an expression of *your* assessment of the situation.

- Good advice can be experienced as manipulative and irritating.
- Good advice can only be given on the basis of your own reality.

APPRECIATIVE COMMUNICATION

There is a difference between acknowledgement and appreciation. Acknowledgement is a sign of respect for the other person's view, which ensures that the other person feels understood. Appreciation means that you value the other person's qualities in such ways that he or she feels appreciated.

Acknowledgement, as well as appreciation, are important elements in the dialogic process.

As described on p. 36, John Gottman has researched the ratio of appreciative and critical responses used by couples who describe themselves as happy and satisfied. He discovered that there was an inexplicably consistent distribution between positive and critical responses. The happy couples would, for example, show:

- five positive responses for each negative response;
- five compliments for each criticism;
- five empathic responses for each outburst of anger.

When we emphasize appreciation in the conversation, it is important to stress that appreciation is not the same as praise or mindless positivity. We disagree completely with the present trend where everything should be oh so positive and smooth, where there is no room for anything negative and critical.

We see this attempted streamlined positivity everywhere – in self-development, child-rearing, coaching, and management philosophy. Here, we are constantly taught that there are no problems – only challenges. *We are supposed to see the opportunities in situations in which we are up to our necks in stress, staff shortage, and bad management.*

Parents are also extremely preoccupied with focusing positively and remembering to praise their children, so they can develop healthy and good self-esteem. For this reason, they praise even the most insignificant spur-of-the-moment drawing which the child brings home from the kindergarten.

At home, many women face the mirror and remind themselves that they are their thoughts – hence they should think positive and good thoughts about themselves. "I am delightful and beautiful," the mantra goes – learnt by heart from a lifestyle magazine. But does that make you more beautiful?

The problem with this kind of praise is that, through it, we attempt to reflect only what we want to see. We attempt to put all the difficult, ugly, and unacceptable issues behind us, as if they did not exist.

In our practice, we tend to oppose this trend. The reason is that we have seen and experienced the degree to which we deprive ourselves of important insights, when we do not face aspects of our own or our partner's view of the world that are negative and critical. We believe that if we do not acknowledge negative outbursts and the frustrations in our lives, then we cut ourselves off from an enormous source of energy and a resource for our personal development.

Yes, we would even go as far as to say that we should focus precisely on criticism and frustration, because the seed for further development and release is found in the longing that lies beneath criticism and frustration.

APPRECIATIVE INQUIRY (AI)

AI is one of the trendy methods that has often been misused and misunderstood as focusing exclusively on positivity. That was not the original intention of AI.

AI, which means acknowledging and appreciative inquiry, is an American concept which was developed during the 1980s, initially as a tool for organizational development. Later, the AI ideas were applied to individual, personal development as a way of practising positive psychology (Cooperider, 2001).

IN ORDER TO MEET ITSELF A SOUL HAS TO MEET ANOTHER SOUL.

- PLATO -

DIALOGUE

When the dialogue stops, the relationship ends! Perhaps it is as simple as that. However, conducting an acknowledging dialogue is a greater challenge than most people realize. Dialogue requires practice, whether you are a psychologist, an engineer, or an actor.

The reason is that a dialogue is more than just a conversation. What we understand by an acknowledging dialogue is a conversation with the purpose of creating understanding through each other's stories and differences. It may sound a little artificial, but, nevertheless, it is important.

In a successful dialogue we explore the world together, and put things into a shared perspective. When we open up and become curious about a topic, then we often experience something unexpected.

So, even if we have been married for twenty-four years, a good dialogue will continue to bring new nuances, realizations, and perceptions of ourselves and each other.

A DIALOGUE OF ACKNOWLEDGEMENT IS CHARACTERIZED BY:

- "risk" of change. In the dialogue we run the risk of understanding things in a new way and thereby having to think and act in new ways;

- there are no right answers. The point of departure is that nobody has the right answers to the questions the dialogue introduces;

- a good ability to listen. A good dialogue requires patience and a willingness to put your own ego on standby.

DIALOGUE KILLERS

It is difficult to maintain a good and meaningful conversation when:

- **we are interrupted**

Sometimes we get started on what we want to say, and then we are interrupted, deflected or distracted. This means that we have to begin telling the same story all over again in our attempt to be heard.

- **the listener is restless**

"Yes, yes, I already heard that." "Please get to the point." "Do I have to listen to those complaints all over again? What else is new?" A great many men cannot be bothered to listen to all the stories many women wish to tell. However, the very same men are often unaware that, by virtue of their rejection, they become active players in conversations which they feel are suffocating, long-winded, and dull. In tennis language, you could say that in many conversations men tend to "hit only three balls". Then they think the match is over. Actually, they want to get the conversation over with quickly and perhaps they even feel it is a waste of time. If you continue this line of communication, you play an extremely active part in the killing of the dialogue. We use the expression that the long road becomes the short road and that the short road may end up becoming the long road.

- **the listener is provoked by difference**

It is important to bear in mind that your partner has a right to think and understand various issues the way they do. "But can't I then also express my disagreement?" you might ask. Yes, and hence it is important to be able to distinguish between agreeing with people and acknowledging other people's right to experience things the way they do. When we agree with other people, we support their views. However, when we acknowledge other people's right to their view, then it does not matter whether or not we agree with them.

- **two people talk and nobody listens**

Many people do not listen, because they are so busy hanging on to what they already know. They can barely wait until the other person has finished talking, so they can either reject or confirm the other person's views. In this way, they seek to convince the other person that their own version of the story, with which they feel at home, is the valid version. When conducting a successful dialogue, you should remain enquiring and curious instead of constantly attempting to convince the other person as to how to "understand the facts". When the conversation partners do not listen, neither contributes to their thought processes with new ideas. They merely rehearse their own prejudices and experience, thereby depriving themselves of the opportunity to develop other perspectives on, and interpretations of, reality.

- **the receiver is only interested in his or her own story**

A common experience in conversation is that we have associations while the other person talks. Hence, we begin to tell our own story as soon as the other person pauses for breath. That is quite disturbing, as we then have to try and keep track of two stories.

As demonstrated above, it is actually rather difficult to remain in a dialogue and not get into a discussion, a trivial conversation, or a fight. The first prerequisite of creating a good dialogue is to be present for the other person. Then we should be able to listen to the other person until he or she has completed their story. It is in this space that undisturbed, deep contact can grow. Some people have waited a lifetime for this close contact and presence in conversation, because it gives them a feeling of being unique. The way we see it is that we do not need to wait any longer. We can take things into our own hands.

THE SUN IS FOOD

CONFLICTS ARE PURE GOLD

W hen clients arrive in our consultation room, cold winds of conflict tend to be blowing in their relationship and neither of the partners can find shelter from the wind.

In our experience, many believe that their partner holds the key to resolving these conflicts. The partner must understand and learn something or other before the relationship can improve. *My partner must change before I can get better and develop . . .*

For this reason, many clients initially look astonished when we tell them that we are not interested in discussing who should change. Our point is we want clients to learn to appreciate their conflicts and welcome their frustrations, because these are the seeds of understanding, reconciliation, and release.

If we attempt to fight criticism and frustrations in our lives, the result will be that we cut ourselves off from an enormous source of energy and development. The energy sustaining our frustrations should, in fact, be used as a starting point for moving beyond the power struggles that wear down so many relationships.

Imagine that your painful experiences from childhood are like a volcano. Like a volcano, they have smouldering layers under the surface, invisible to the naked eye. However, from time to time, lava spurts from the interior. Our outpourings of criticism, frustration, or anger are experienced by the other person as scorn, threats, or humiliations. All the emotional lava has one thing in common; it stems from the bedrock of old experiences.

By using the Dialogue of Acknowledgement, we gain insight into the nature of these experiences and longings. We might, for instance, long for something we needed in childhood, but never received. We might long for consolation that never arrived after a frightening experience, for understanding that we never received after a distressing event that was beyond our control.

Gradually, the shouting, the dislike, the hurt, or the disagreements that the couple may experience might give way to memories of what these conflict situations remind us of. And, little by little, we begin to be able to piece together our story of what this trouble is all about.

When working with frustration and criticism, the codeword is longing. The reason is that behind every recurring criticism lurks a frustration, and behind that we find a longing on the part of the person who is expressing the criticism. The frustration or the criticism is not the important issue.

The important issue is to understand the underlying longing and what it reminds us of.

One could say that 90% of a criticism or a frustration belongs to early experiences of the person criticizing or expressing frustrations. Only 10% is directly related to their partner's behaviour!

This realization is essential. By learning to express the longing embedded in the criticism, we can transform the power struggle into something positive and productive.

"IT IS NOT DIFFICULT TO GET ANGRY. ANYONE CAN GET ANGRY. IT IS, HOWEVER, A FINE ART TO BECOME ANGRY WITH THE RIGHT PERSON IN THE RIGHT WAY, AT THE RIGHT TIME – AND FOR THE RIGHT REASON."

– ARISTOTLE –

BEHIND EVERY CRITICISM THERE IS A LONGING

For many years, we have had a recurrent conflict when travelling by car. Using the Dialogue of Acknowledgement, we have arrived at some new discoveries that enable us to respect each other's feelings better. We are now also able to joke about our differing views on safe driving.

We are on the way from the island of Langeland, where we live, to our clinic in Copenhagen. Piet is driving and Kirsten is sitting next to him. We are going at a high speed and not many words are exchanged. After some kilometres Kirsten explodes, "You are driving too fast and you do not keep a safe distance to the other cars." Piet slows down a little. Once again, Kirsten has criticized his driving. Piet's first reaction is anger. Kirsten's statement that he is not a good driver quite simply makes him furious, since he is actually a good driver, and he tells her so. Afterwards, he is sorry and withdraws, because the criticism makes him feel somewhat alone and that she is dissatisfied with him. This happens time and time again. A bad atmosphere is the result, when the two partners each pull in their direction.

One day, during a Dialogue of Acknowledgement about this issue, Kirsten begins to talk about her fear when Piet drives at a high speed. At this point some underlying issues begin to surface.

Kirsten recalls how frightened she was as a child during her daily trips by car with her father from North Zealand to Copenhagen, where she went to school. Her father was always speeding, and he crossed the intersections without slowing down. Kirsten remembers how afraid she was on that trip every single time and how her father thought that her fear was a lot of nonsense. Kirsten felt neither seen nor heard – a feature that characterized her entire upbringing, Her mother and father, each in their own ways, were unable to contain her strong feelings. As a result, she was often perceived as a somewhat hysterical child.

In her adult life, Kirsten has always been afraid of making Piet angry. Because Kirsten has never really learned to handle strong feelings, she attempts to avoid provoking Piet's anger. In the car example above, Kirsten resorts to her old defence. She attempts to close off or wear the "Madonna smile". However, now and then, in the heat of the moment, she begins to shout about speeding tickets and speed-crazy drivers. The result is never good.

When Piet begins to tell first about his anger and then about his sadness, he taps into his old memories about his father criticizing him and always being able to handle things better than him.

Piet recognizes his old pattern of closing off and handling everything himself.

Because we started to tell our stories, listen, and understand each other and see the situation in the car in a completely different light, our car journeys changed radically. We now always agree to leave at least fifteen minutes early in order to be in good time. Furthermore, we bring tea along, so that we can take a break on the way. This strategy works wonders. Kirsten now begins to comment on speed in a new way, where she also signals her state of mind. "Oh dear, I am getting my speed anxiety again . . . could we please go just a little bit slower." Piet is now able to contain the comments on his driving, because they are no longer a personal negative attack, which he needs to defend himself against.

Exploring the conflict had a positive result. We entered into a constructive dialogue. Kirsten dared to protest. It hurt Piet a little, but the silence would have hurt him more. Kirsten experienced being taken seriously. The atmosphere in the car cooled down and we both experience a deeper connection.

Kirsten and Piet

BEFORE THE DIALOGUE OF ACKNOWLEDGEMENT

T he Dialogue of Acknowledgement has not just turned out to be extremely useful to couples. It can also be used with great effect between parents and children, between friends, and in the workplace. Its big strength is that it provides the confidence that is the most important precondition for a couple's return to respectful and nurturing ways of sharing each other's worlds.

The Dialogue of Acknowledgement is the fundamental framework of a number of other dialogues for couples that we practise in our therapy with couples. We have seen very many examples of the way this dialogue functions well for couples in crisis.

In addition, the Dialogue of Acknowledgement offers new ways to establish mutual understanding in efficient and gentle ways. The dialogue is particularly suitable when we wish to communicate something to our partner, or if we wish to change something in our relationship with regard to the raising of children, money matters, jealousy, our mother-in-law, or sexuality.

THE ACTUAL DIALOGUE

The Dialogue of Acknowledgement consists of three steps:

- THE MIRRORING PROCESS
- ACKNOWLEDGEMENT
- EMPATHY

THE MIRRORING PROCESS

The cornerstone of relational thinking is the mirroring process. This unique way of communicating is the distinguishing characteristic of relational therapy, as opposed to other schools of therapy for couples.

The mirroring process consists in active listening, where the listener reflects as precisely as possible the contents of a message from the partner (the person telling his or her story).

The purpose of the mirroring process is to create a secure framework, in which we can learn more about each other's worlds. The mirroring process allows us to be seen for who we really are and to flourish in each other's presence.

The actual mirroring process is as follows:

- the couple makes a choice as to who should listen and who should tell his or her story. The storyteller should be the person who has a conflict or a troublesome feeling that he or she would like to explore;

- in a few precise sentences, the storyteller explains the problem. The storyteller begins with one or two sentences: for example, "*I would like to tell you about . . .*" It is important that the speaker uses the pronoun I and does not blame the partner or use ungracious language;

- the listener repeats as closely as possible the words of the storyteller and begins with the words: "*What I hear you saying is that . . .*" It is important not to interpret, add, subtract, nor enhance any aspects of the story told.

- the listener concludes with the words: "*Was that the gist of what you said?*" Or: "*Did I miss out on anything?*";

- if the listener forgot something, the storyteller repeats his or her version;

- the listener mirrors the storyteller again, until the storyteller feels completely heard. When that happens, the listener asks: *"Is there more? Please tell me more!"*;

- the storyteller shares further descriptions of his or her problem or emotion. It is still important to be brief, stick to the subject, and not go off on a tangent;

- the listener reflects the storyteller and concludes with the words: *"Was that what you said?"*;

- the mirroring process continues in this way without either of the partners interrupting each other, until the storyteller feels that the aspects of his or her problem or particular emotion have been explored and mirrored;

- when the storyteller feels that the theme is fully dealt with, the listener gives a summary of the contents, beginning with the words: *"The essence of what I heard you say is . . ."*

- the listener ends his or her summary with the words: *"Is this a good enough summary?"*

In the beginning, the mirroring process can seem like artificial parroting. Nevertheless, our advice is to get started and apply the same enthusiasm as when we begin to learn to play an instrument. At first it sounds shrill and monotonous, but then you grasp the technique and the tunes begin to take shape.

We are likely to have the same experience when we begin to apply the mirroring process as a method. Most of us need to practise before we experience the desired effect. The effect consists in a gentle mirroring process that enables us to see ourselves more clearly, in a new perspective, and with new insights. Equally profound can be the experience that the partner, who is mirroring our story, is suddenly – as if by magic – able to identify with our story and understand what we are saying and feeling.

Unfortunately, some people never get to the point where they have this incredibly moving experience of being seen and heard as the people they really are. This should be a human right.

When the mirroring process works as efficiently as described above, it is because the person who is doing the mirroring is able to enter into the process and be fully attentive and present. When the storyteller's issues are not just heard and repeated, but listened to, taken in, and mirrored with acknowledgement and complete empathy and understanding, the connection is made – a feeling that could be described with the words: *now we are suddenly back in tune. Right now we understand each other. Right now I dare open up again. Right now . . .*

RELEASE

"During the mirroring process I suddenly felt that we entered a flow where we unexpectedly shared a language, communicating one soul to another. It was deeply moving to feel the strength of our being there for one another. It was as if the light suddenly broke through and a personal release took place. Something touched us on a deeper level. Something extremely authentic, which I had not felt between us for many years. I felt a large lump in my throat, and the tears rolled down my cheeks. It was a strange mixture of great pain and happiness. But most of all it had a great releasing effect on us. While we sat there holding hands and looking into each other's eyes, the deadlock, the bitterness, and the strain were suddenly released."

Hedvig

THE NATURE OF THE MIRRORING PROCESS

As we have mentioned, an astonishing number of issues in our adult lives originate in our early childhood. Often, we are unaware of this.

A child develops its identity by being mirrored by adults. This happens from birth, as the baby discovers the world and begins to develop a self by exploring its mother's facial expressions. That is also the explanation for the completely instinctual and unconscious reflex all mothers have when they mirror the facial expressions of their baby.

Whether the baby's face wrinkles, when they cry or light up in giant smiles, we unconsciously mirror the baby's facial expressions. When the child sees itself in its mother's face, as it were, it is having the first experiences of its own identity. These mirroring processes generate neural networks in the baby's brain. These neural connections enable the child to develop a sense of self.

Infants need a vibrant, expressive face and closeness that can calm them down when they are agitated. When a confident connection has been established between mother and child, the child gradually develops an ability to regulate him- or herself.

The mirroring process is vital if babies are to thrive. Since the mirroring process is so fundamental to infant health, we venture to assume that the confidence and nurturing generated by the mirroring process continue to be crucial even when we are adults. This assumption is supported by our experiences with relational therapy (Stern, 1985).

THE LISTENER'S RESPONSIBILITY

It is not always easy to enter into the mirroring process. Sometimes, we cannot remember or relate what the storyteller has said. This is quite all right.

The American psychologist Hedy Schleifer says that, *at the edge of possible growth sits the angel of forgetfulness and says, Please repeat what you just said!* Hence, it is not embarrassing to ask to hear everything again. There might even be a deeper reason as to why we need to hear the story a couple of times.

The listener also faces the major challenge of not retreating into his or her own world. There might be many reasons as to why it can be difficult to listen to what the storyteller says without having the opportunity to speak. Here, it might be a good idea to remember that 90% of a criticism or a frustration belongs to early experiences of the person criticizing or expressing frustrations. Only 10% is directly related to their partner's behaviour! So, even if the listener is perhaps the releasing factor, the story primarily derives from the storyteller. This understanding enables the listener to stay present and respond to the story told with curiosity and interest.

The listener's responsibility is to be attentive and refrain from expressing his or her own thoughts and emotions in the process. This is easier said than done in the heat of an argument when our blood is boiling and our pulse rate is 220, because we may find the story told extremely provoking. It is precisely at this point that the storyteller needs the listener's continued presence the most. It is at precisely this point that the listener has the responsibility to make an ethical choice to stay present without responding.

The last thing the storyteller needs is that the listener explodes (again!). As the listener, you have the option of saying:

– *"What I hear you say is that . . ."*; *"Please tell me more . . ."*; *"Was there something I missed?"*; *"Is there more?"*

The listener should not:

- ask questions;
- interpret what is being said;
- consider some of the issues related as important and others as less important;
- bring in his or her own new words.

Because we constantly attempt to create meaning based on our own world view, interpretation is tempting to the listener. However, when we mirror, it is not allowed to bring our own interpretations or our own new words and priorities into the process. We call it "illegal import of own material" into the other person's country. It is a major challenge for most people to refrain from "importing" and leave their own thoughts and associations for a while in order to concentrate fully on their partner.

THE STORYTELLER'S RESPONSIBILITY

The storyteller focuses on his or her own story and tells it as briefly and as precisely as possible in the first person singular. The storyteller must avoid criticism and derision of the partner.

It is a dialogical process, even if it is structured. Your partner is just as active as you and is hard at work listening. Hence, he or she should be recognized by the way he or she listens to your story without interrupting apart from the mirroring. Afterwards, you might comment, *"You got most of it. What I would also like you to hear is that . . ."*

In this part of the dialogue it is easy to fail. It seems easy, but as mentioned, it can get very difficult.

Don't worry, the listener's turn will come!

ACKNOWLEDGEMENT

When the mirroring process of the storyteller's problem or experience has been completed, the listener proceeds to acknowledge what he or she has just heard. Here, we are talking about a process in which the listener tells the storyteller that everything that he or she has said makes sense.

Acknowledgement is about conveying an understanding of the storyteller's problem and story by placing yourself in his or her position and seeing the world temporarily from his or her perspective.

A client once described listening with acknowledgement and then, later, empathy as a process of putting all your thoughts into a balloon and leaving it floating in the air so that in this way we are fully available to the other person's thoughts and nothing else.

Here, we are not talking about agreeing on an interpretation of reality. Even if a couple talks about the same thing, there will always be at least two ways of seeing the same issue.

Here, we begin a very exciting process; a dance where we are gradually released from the shadows of our childhood. This process will allow us to gain a more accurate idea of the person whom we married.

EMPATHY

The third and last step is empathy, where the listener again should try to place him- or herself in the partner's world – this time emotionally. At this stage, the listener shows his or her empathy by describing how he or she imagines that the storyteller feels about the story that has just been told.

Here, the listener attempts to imagine how the story told must have affected the storyteller. When the storyteller listens to the suggested feelings, the storyteller becomes more aware of how he or she actually feels.

Empathy is always guesswork. We cannot know how the other person feels. However, we do attempt to imagine feelings, which we presume are connected with the issues in the story we have been told.

ROUNDING OFF AND MUTUAL APPRECIATION

When nothing more needs to be said, we remain seated for a little while, sensing how the partners feel "the space in between". In time, we may begin to look at this space in between as the place where we attempt to create a good intimate atmosphere with confidence. We might also see it as a playground, where we can play together.

The dialogue concludes with a mutual appreciation of the partners' contribution to the session.

SWITCHING ROLES

At this point we might reverse the process, with the listener becoming the storyteller and the storyteller becoming the listener, and continue the dialogue on the same theme.

WORTH KNOWING BEFORE YOU GET STARTED

TAKING TURNS

In the Dialogue of Acknowledgement there is always one person who tells a story and one who listens and mirrors. When two people speak simultaneously or when two people are silent together, there is no dialogue. A prerequisite for hearing each other's story is that we create a calm atmosphere. Taking turns means that we alternate being the person talking and the person listening and this is a wonderful way to create a calm atmosphere.

The storyteller's challenge is to tell his or her story in an authentic way, while also maintaining contact with the listener.

The listener's challenge is to be there 100% for the person who is talking, resisting the temptation to fall back into his or her own thoughts and emotions. It can, however, also be a relief to know that *all I have to do is to listen and mirror.*

CHOICE OF THEME

The dialogue begins when the couple settles on a theme they wish to talk about. If one of the partners has invited the other to a dialogue with a specific theme, then there is no problem.

If, however, the couple has reserved time for a dialogue only if they are in therapy for couples, the mirroring process begins by both participants identifying a theme or subject they would like to explore. The subject may be something they find difficult, or something that creates problems in the relationship, and the couple might want to investigate why the problems occur.

When the couple has settled on a range of themes, they should select one of them. The choice also involves one of the partners choosing the storyteller's role and the other person the listener's role. The couple first decides who takes which roles for this dialogue. If there is time and energy, the couple may select another theme later, and when the dialogue is complete they then reverse positions.

THE GIFTS OF SLOW PACE AND SILENCE

The distinguishing characteristics of this type of dialogue are time and pace.

It is necessary to be aware of the advantages of maintaining a slow pace in dialogue. There should be time for being thoughtful and in touch with feelings. With a slow pace and the accompanying silence, insights come little by little, as old memories surface. Silence is golden, when it is natural. During silence, it often happens that surprising new memories, emotions, and thoughts surface. When we are caught up in a flow of free associations, and our curious and empathic partner is sitting in front of us listening, then we have an opportunity to enter uncharted territory and explore together.

It follows that our bodily experience is also affected by the calm and the silence. Suddenly, we may feel and sense our bodies in ways which we only rarely experience. We have the opportunity to "feel" our thoughts and their presence in our bodies – important sensations that can help us get in touch with childhood memories that we have hitherto not matched with words and pictures.

Bodily sensations can be experienced in the chest region, as "a knot in the stomach", or a diffuse sensation of unease. We may then attempt to relate these sensations to prior experiences, either in adulthood or from our childhood. This detective work can help us understand and tell stories that accompany the feelings of grief, anxiety, or frustration with which we began the dialogue.

In this way, it becomes possible to get in touch with the longing that always lurks behind any frustration. By exploring this longing, we can re-establish the confidence and the closeness that are at the core of the puzzle.

Another special aspect of the Acknowledging Dialogue is that even if it often seems that our partner is the "cause" of our frustration, it is now suddenly evident – eureka – that it is him or her who can be our close and confident helper. In the beginning, this can only be done by using the clear structure of the Acknowledging Dialogue. However, as we progress, we will find that a sense of security spreads through all our emotional levels and we may feel more secure when talking with our partner about difficult issues.

EYE CONTACT

The Dialogue of Acknowledgement is not just a dialogue that you begin in random ways with an arbitrary subject. Because the Dialogue of Acknowledgement should unfold in structured ways, it also has its own "prelude" and "stage setting".

The "prelude" is an invitation to a dialogue and making a mutual agreement as to when it should take place and what it should be about. The "stage setting" consists of a space in which the participants face each other, with knees and hands able to touch, during the dialogue.

In fact, we are trying to create a magical distance. This is a distance that enables us to have a special contact and physical intimacy. As infants we loved this intimacy, when we met our mother's gaze, and felt her close as she held us in her arms.

Anyone who has held an infant in his or her arms knows that there is a certain distance at which there is an optimal opportunity for profound and intimate eye contact. As parents, we instinctively adjust the angles of our heads, hands, and arms to position them at this magical distance, where children and adults can linger peacefully in each others' gaze.

Facing each other at this distance with a deep eye contact is an excellent exercise for adults. It helps us to re-learn how to linger safely in close contact and find peace and quiet in the process.

This particular position, where we face each other, initiates a new process. It is quite natural. However, as we know, all learning can be difficult, but it is important just to hang in there. In time, this particular position will generate confidence and curiosity, the effect of which will be that it no longer feels exhausting. Sometimes, you might even long for a couple of minutes of absolute silence with deep eye contact with your partner.

Usually, we are not conscious of the fact that our brain is also participating. Wordless eye contact initiates cerebral processes that are beneficial to us, such as the profound reciprocity, calm, and joy that we experience when we have deep eye contact with an infant.

In a relationship on thin ice, where the two partners are at odds, it might be painful and almost impossible to maintain eye contact. This is precisely why this "stage setting" is particularly important, since it helps to repair and reinforce a new but fragile development between two battered partners.

Moreover, people who have grown up with an insecure attachment style may, in general, have problems maintaining deep eye contact. However, working intentionally on difficult issues will also lead to healing of old pain in these situations.

THE SPACE IN BETWEEN

When profound eye and soul contact have been established, the time has come to explore and sense the "space" between the partners, who are now sitting close and facing each other.

This is the shared space in which we will work on improving our relationship. It is also the shared space in which we live and breathe on a daily basis. "The space in between" consists of all the things we share – all the things we say and do, and which, for these reasons, are decisive in terms of creating a nice or an unpleasant shared space. Even if one of the partners is at work and the other is at home, there is still a shared space, an emotional connection between the partners, which can be influenced at a distance.

When we meet a couple who have a good relationship we may be aware that the reason it is pleasant for us to be in their company is that they have a special bond – we feel the secure, fertile space they share.

When we are at odds with one another, the "space in between" is not a particularly pleasant place to be for either the couple or their children. It is important that we protect this shared space by understanding that we cannot fill it with all kinds of negative issues without incurring major consequences. The Dialogue of Acknowledgement might for a time build a healthy awareness of the mutual responsibility for this vital shared space. In this way, we might help the space to grow in a positive sense.

APPRECIATION

When we wish to address various issues in our relationship, it is important to recognize aspects of our relationship that work well. Similarly, when we have to talk about difficult issues that may involve conflict, then it is a really good idea to begin to focus on the areas where there are no problems.

For this reason, the Dialogue of Acknowledgement always begins with a mutual appreciation in which we express appreciation of those of our partner's traits which give us pleasure. It may be something our partner has said or done, or a contribution he or she made lately.

In general, we tend to appreciate the good things in life too little. Why should we only voice our appreciation of each other at our important wedding anniversaries, or at our fortieth or fiftieth birthdays? We can never receive enough appreciation, and hence we begin and end the Dialogue of Acknowledgement with mutual appreciation.

What I appreciate about you right now is that . . .

One partner tells what he or she appreciates and then the other partner mirrors the appreciation as closely as possible. Then you switch roles.

THE BRIDGE

After appreciation, there is again a focus on the "space in between". Imagine a small bridge from one partner to the other. The bridge is so small that it only allows for the passage of one person at a time. We can take turns opening our doors and leaving our secure home, walking on to the bridge to the other person's door, and getting invited in. This is a metaphor for how we may visit each other's reality.

But is this not a little complicated and contrived? Do I really need to visit via a small imaginary bridge? I know my husband through and through. I know everything about him.

Nothing could be further from the truth. We may, if we so desire, visit each other throughout our lives and gain new insights, new angles, and new experiences in each other's company.

For this reason, we should attempt to bring our curiosity and openness along and cross the bridge to our partner in order to visit his or her innermost world, reality, and past in a new way.

Some of the major challenges in this crossing are the strong forces that, every now and again, want to pull us back into our own worlds. While we make the greatest effort to listen to and be near our partner, the stories will stimulate thoughts, emotions, and impulses that can draw us back to our own world.

The reason is that the listener usually has a "Yes, but . . . animal" on his or her shoulder who constantly needs attention. *No, it was not like that. No, I did not say that. Don't you think it was more like . . . Do you really believe that that did not hurt me?*

The "Yes, but . . . animal" must be kept on a short leash by the listener. If the partner feels that the listener is not completely attentive, he or she might not open up and share vulnerable issues.

Keeping our "Yes, but . . . animals" from interfering is easier said than done. Occasionally, an intense dialogue may take place inside the listener's head on the subject of "wanting to go home" to defend him or herself. The internal dialogue might be so disturbing that the listener cannot concentrate or hear directly what the partner is saying.

When the listener is fighting to maintain his or her position on the bridge, then we cannot assume that this goes unnoticed by the partner. Because we are facing each other, our partner will immediately read the look in our eyes and intuitively know if there is a lack of genuine commitment in our presence.

If this occurs, it is important that the listener says, "I unintentionally returned to my world. I am so sorry. I will revisit you in a minute."

CAN WE REALLY DO THIS?

Perhaps we are asking ourselves if we are actually able to go through with all this, if we can remember it and dare to go all the way!

Anyone who has the will and the courage to throw him- or herself into this experience with sincerity and openness can do it. Just consider that once we all mastered the intimate dialogue and shared great freedom and confidence. Otherwise, we would never have become a couple. We just have to find that place of intimacy again. So, why not be the first to take the chance to retrieve that intimacy? At the beginning, it might feel awkward and contrived to work in such scheduled and structured ways with issues that are so sensitive and difficult to handle. However, we will soon realize that precisely because of the structure and because the mirroring process inspires completely new thoughts, a couple will experience the unspeakable joy of being listened to with the intense attention we all dream of getting. We may also experience that we find new safe ground where we can begin to change the difficult issues in our lives, so that a new insight and a new way of being together can emerge.

If it is too difficult to handle the process alone, there is always the option of continuing the work with a therapist, who is trained to use the dialogic tools. The therapist can be the prime facilitator, who can teach you how to use the Dialogue of Acknowledgement in your daily life.

THE DIALOGUE OF ACKNOWLEDGEMENT

The storyteller tells his or her story and the listener mirrors the words, makes a summary, acknowledges, and expresses empathy.

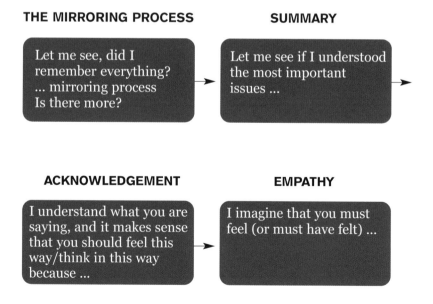

THE MIRRORING PROCESS

Let me see, did I remember everything? ... mirroring process Is there more?

SUMMARY

Let me see if I understood the most important issues ...

ACKNOWLEDGEMENT

I understand what you are saying, and it makes sense that you should feel this way/think in this way because ...

EMPATHY

I imagine that you must feel (or must have felt) ...

WE NOW HAVE A SHARED LANGUAGE

Using the Acknowledging Dialogue from time to time yields significant results. It establishes a connection unlike any other techniques. I get in touch with Philip's soul and this connection creates a completely new atmosphere in our relationship. It is easier for me to stay present when we fight and I am able to tackle our crises in new ways. Otherwise, I tend to go on to autopilot and shut down. There is greater respect and acknowledgement in the space between us. Our good experiences increase and become more nourishing, and the result is that our relationship becomes more fun for me. I get the courage to tell Philip how I feel also in difficult situations; the courage to be present in the moment.

I also experience the importance of the fact that we now have a shared language. When I am invited to Philip's place, I am grateful that I am "allowed" to be in his place 100% and see him as he really is; I see him in new ways even if we have been together for eleven years. I become aware of new aspects of myself and of Philip. I also realize that Philip can be a resource, helping me to become less confused about my personal issues.

I experience the Acknowledging Dialogue as very simple and easy to embrace. In the process, I often "return to my own world", but that is fine. When I succeed in crossing the bridge I enjoy visiting Philip. I get a new understanding of him, which in turn creates a new understanding between us.

Sidsel

OUR GOOD LIVES HAVE GROWN

I am very enthusiastic about the Dialogue of Acknowl-edgement, since it creates a space where prejudices are not allowed. Here I can be myself and say just what I want to say, because I know that Sidsel is "only" supposed to listen and repeat my words. Sidsel is not responsible for what I say. The mirroring process makes it crystal clear that I alone have the responsibility for my life. When Sidsel mirrors my words, I begin to think about what I have just said. This has a fantastic effect on me and I get a better grip on what I actually mean. I get a better understanding of my behaviour and the reasons why I do the things I do.

In relation to Sidsel, the dialogical mirroring process also gives me a realization of the fact that I am 50% of our relationship and therefore have considerable influence on how our lives might unfold. I can control how wonderful our life together could be. When I dare to be 100% present and participate actively in our relationship, then the bonds between us are greatly reinforced and our love doesn't just grow – it virtually blooms.

I actually like the simplicity of the technique. It "only" requires the full presence of both partners. I do not have to consider my choice of words or the sequence in which I want to talk about my issues. It calms down my brain and my mind. It is a relief when my mind relaxes and it becomes my turn to listen to Sidsel, repeat what she just said, and refrain from interpretation!

When I participate in a dialogic mirroring process with Sidsel I have a unique experience of being present here and now in the moment.

Philip

THE LOGBOOK
OF THE SHIP
"HENRY DAVID THOREAU"

THE
TRUT H

ALWAYS
HAPPEПS

AFGEGEVEN 1 AUG. 1970

77

ZeSdE BoEk
THE KING OF
SUMMER

THE DIALOGUE OF ACKNOWLEDGEMENT STEP BY STEP

THE PREPARATION

1. Find two comfortable chairs facing each other. Position yourselves with 50 cm (20 inches) between your faces. Place your feet firmly on the ground and let your hands rest on your thighs. Do not clench your hands. When our hands are open, we are more in touch with our state of mind at this point in time.

2. Sink into the chair and feel what it is like to be where you are. If you want to, then join hands. Maintaining physical contact with each other contributes much to the dialogue.

Holding hands becomes increasingly natural as the dialogue process progresses.

EYE CONTACT

3. Look each other in the eye. It is important to maintain eye contact until your thoughts begin to settle and find a pace where you are able to be present and receptive to your partner. Try looking at each other with the curiosity of a child. Let yourself explore with "soft baby eyes". Remind yourselves that your full presence is a gift to the other.

APPRECIATION

4. Now we should take some deep breaths and let our curiosity develop into appreciation. Even when we are at odds with each other, there is always something positive to say to our partner. Remember that if we are constantly faced with criticism and demands we will never be able to open up. The minute we create security for one another by appreciating each other, we can let down our guard.

We could, for instance, say:

Thank you for bringing me breakfast in bed this morning.
Thank you for being in my life.

I am so glad that you . . .
*I appreciate you for your courage to go through the difficult times
with me. You have a special significance in my life.*

CHOICE OF THEME

5. Now it is time to tell each other about the themes you would
like to work with. Then you should decide who should be the
storyteller and who should be the listener. The storyteller has a
theme he or she would like to explore and now it is the storyteller's task to take the listener on a journey into this topic.

THE SPACE AND THE BRIDGE

6. At this point you should gradually move into the space
between one another. How does the space we inhabit together
feel now? Take your time to answer.

7. Imagine the bridge between your two worlds. It is a small thin
bridge, where there is only room for one person at a time. Where
on the bridge are you standing?

8. When one of you is ready, the storyteller invites the partner,
the listener, for a dialogue. Take your time.

The storyteller: *I would like to invite you into my world so that
you can hear what I want to say to you.*

9. Now the listener imagines that he or she crosses the bridge to
the partner's world. This means leaving his or her own well-
known world with all its baggage. We bring only a passport and a
visa for entry. We are now ready to enter the partner's world with
sincere curiosity and enthusiasm. Only then will it be possible for
you to get to know your partner's world, language, and culture.
Buddhists call this the "beginner's mind"; we are ready to listen
and embark on a mirroring process with eyes, ears, mouth, heart,
and body.

10. Remember to focus continually on deep breathing, which relaxes body and mind. The deep breathing will create space inside each of us.

11. The Listener

The mirroring process begins when we invite our partner to tell us about his or her theme. *I would really like to hear something about . . .*

12. The Storyteller

Step by step, you should now give an authentic account of the frustration or the theme you have selected. *I am really concerned about . . .*

You begin by describing your frustration or your theme. What is it about, when does it occur, and in what connection? What emotions accompany the theme, and what behaviour does it generate? It is important not to control or censor the material that is emerging. Remember that you are in a phase of discovery. Hence, it is important that you say whatever comes to mind. Try also to find a rhythm so the sentences become precise and not too long. This gives the listener a chance to engage with the mirroring process as fluently as possible.

13. The Listener

You should constantly make sure that you mirror everything that the storyteller tells you, and preferably use his or her choice of words as much as possible. When we mirror our partner's language in a precise manner, we become more aware of his or her preferred ways of expression. Through this process we will gradually and almost imperceptibly move still closer to our partner's world. Take your time to look at your partner prior to the mirroring process. Really take in your partner. Read in your partner's face what your presence does to him or her and end every mirroring process with the words: *Did I get everything?*

Then you should continue with the words: *Please tell me more,* or *Is there more to tell?*

If you cannot remember what to mirror, you just say: *Will you please tell me again?*

If you happen to "run back across the bridge" to your own world, then remember to tell your partner. You could, for instance, say, *I did a home run, but now I am back here with you.*

SUMMARY

14. The Listener
Gives a short summary of what the storyteller has said and concludes with the words: *Did I get the most important issues?* or *Was this summary all right?*

15. The Storyteller
Confirms or disconfirms that the essential issues have been heard.

16. The Listener
Continues the mirroring process until all the essential issues are included.

ACKNOWLEDGEMENT

17. The Listener
Acknowledges that he or she has understood the storyteller's story. The point is not to agree with what has been said, but that the listener conveys that he or she sees the world with his or her partner's eyes.

The listener may, for instance, begin by saying:

It makes sense to me that . . .
I understand that you have experienced these issues in the way you just told me . . .
When I see things from your perspective, I understand that . . .

If there is something that the listener has not understood, then the listener could say:

What I do not quite understand is . . .
Please help me understand . . .

Then the listener summarizes the main points of what the storyteller said and concludes with the words: *Do you feel that I have understood you?*

18. The Storyteller
Confirms that he or she feels understood.

EMPATHY

19. The Listener
May, for instance, say:
I imagine that your story has made you feel . . . (Use only the 2–3 best words that describe the feeling . . .)

20. The Storyteller
Mirrors the emotions suggested by the listener to describe his or her experience.

21. The Listener
Asks: *Are there any more emotions?*

CONCLUSION

22. The Storyteller
Adds any other feelings he or she has in relation to this experience.

23. Sharing
Remain seated for a while and sense what the space between us feels like now. You should remember to maintain eye contact and to keep your hands open. Which emotions can you now use to describe the space – the climate – between you? Think and feel again or say it out loud.

Concluding appreciation
24. The dialogue concludes with mutual appreciation by both the listener and the storyteller.

THE OTHER PARTNER'S TURN

25. If need be, you may take turns and invite your partner to continue the dialogue on the same theme. This time, the storyteller and the listener switch roles.

SIDSEL AND PHILIP

Sidsel and Philip are in their late thirties. They have known each other for eleven years. They share three children, two of their own and one of Sidsel's from a previous relationship. Sidsel and Philip have interesting jobs and are socially involved. They have decided to give their marriage some of the attention which, until now, children and work have demanded relentlessly. Shortly before the dialogue that follows, they attended a seminar for couples at our Relationship Therapy Centre (see also p. 222).

Sidsel's knee touches Philip's chair. There is approximately 50 cm (20 inches) between their faces. They open their hands. Gradually, they take each other's hands and begin to look into each other's eyes. They sit quietly and rest in each other's gaze.

Sidsel is touched and smiles disarmingly. Philip returns the smile. Sidsel begins her appreciation of Philip:

Sidsel
Thank you for your courage and determination in doing this with me.

Philip (begins the mirroring process)
You appreciate my courage and my determination in doing this with you.

Philip continues
I appreciate your great strength and wisdom.

Sidsel
You appreciate my great strength and wisdom

WHO SHOULD VISIT WHOM?

Some time goes by; they gaze at each other, examining each other's moods. Time passes. They smile a little. Then Philip says:

I have something I would like to talk to you about.

Sidsel
I am ready.

Philip
I would like to invite you into my world because there is something important I would like to tell you.

Sidsel takes her time, her gaze is soft, but intense, and she repeats:

I am ready to listen.

Philip
I have an important issue. It is related to the fact that everything I do should always be OK.

Sidsel
You have an important issue related to the fact that everything you do should always be OK.

Philip
Yes, it takes up so much space when I feel that I am not good enough.

Sidsel
I did not quite understand. Would you please repeat?

Philip
I am saying that I occasionally feel that I am not OK. When I have that feeling I doubt whether the things I say and do are all right. That feeling takes up a lot of time and energy.

Sidsel
Not feeling OK and doubting whether what you do is all right take up a lot of your time and energy. Did I miss anything?

Philip
You got it. I am sick and tired of having to check with everybody just prior to doing something.

Philip sighs deeply. He is really frustrated about this issue.

Sidsel
You say that you are sick and tired of always having to check everything out.

Philip
Yes, I don't know why I often look for other people's acceptance of what I do. I'm scared by it.

Sidsel
You are scared that you often search for other people's acceptance, although you know that you are OK. Did I hear you correctly?

Philip
You heard me very well, but it is important that you understand that I always go looking for other people's acceptance of what I do – asking them even if deep down inside I know that what I do is OK. I cannot understand why I do this.

Sidsel
You always look for other people's acceptance and seek their answer even if you know that what you do is quite OK. You cannot understand why you do this. Tell me more!

Philip
When I do it, I see myself as little Philip looking for my mother's acceptance. I also hear her saying: You must do it like this and not like that. Then I become incredibly focused on what I should do or not do. I am so fed up with this.

Sidsel
You increasingly see that you . . . (stops herself) *No, now I think I am doing an interpretation of what you just said. Would you mind telling me that again?*

Philip
Yes, I can see what I did when I was a little boy and my mother always told me what to do. I always tried to please her, get her acceptance and approval.

Sidsel
You see yourself as boy Philip who would do everything your mother told you to do. You did everything to please her and get her acceptance and approval. Was that what it was like?

Philip
Yes, precisely, and I feel so powerless when I, even as an adult, get caught up in this pattern, when my mother says: why don't you do that or stop doing that – it is so ridiculous. I feel so sad. I punish myself, scold myself and tell myself to just ask her to stop. But in reality I do not.

Sidsel
You punish yourself when . . . (stops herself) *no, please repeat what you just said.*

Philip
Two weeks ago I visited my mother and we talked about my idea of importing tea. She just thinks it is a ridiculous project without rhyme or reason. I got caught up in her rejection of my project and felt discouraged. Granted, there would be a lot of money at stake, but I also know that it would be a fantastic project. On top of everything else it could also be fun.

Sidsel
Two weeks ago you visited your mother and she said that your project of selling tea was ridiculous. You felt caught up in her rejection, because there is a lot of money at stake. Still, you feel that it is a fantastic chance, a good project, and on top of everything else it could also be fun. Is there more?

Philip
Even if this project might be far-fetched, I hate myself for so obviously needing my mother's acceptance before committing to it. If I should die with that tea project, then I want to bloody well die standing up . . . (Philip's voice becomes forceful, the tone is angry).

In the same forceful voice as Philip's, Sidsel says:
You hate yourself for needing your mother's acceptance of your

tea project. If you are to die with that project, you want to
bloody well die standing up. Is there more?

(Philip "tastes" Sidsel's mirroring process and then he says):
It is actually nice to feel that if I were to die with that tea project,
then I would want to bloody well die standing up.

Sidsel
It feels nice for you to say that if you should die with this tea
project, then you would want to die standing up. If there is
more, then I am ready.

Philip reflects. There is more.
Right now I experience that it was really good to come here today
and take the lead. Especially the fact that I did not have to ask
anyone's permission. That I just did what was good for me. I am
also glad that I chose to talk about this emotion, that I made it
mine . . .

Sidsel
Coming here and being here feels right. It is wonderful not having
to ask anyone. You feel it is nice to do something for yourself, for
instance by beginning to talk about your issue. You conquered it.

Philip
Yes, I am actually sitting here celebrating it.
Philip chuckles.

Sidsel also laughs and says slowly:
You are celebrating it.
She has a roguish glint in her eyes, which are also full of great
affection.
Is there more you want to say?

Philip
No. At first he answers in a quiet voice and then he repeats loud
and clear:
NO

THE AMOUNT OR VOLUME OF NOISE IS IN AN INVERSE RELATIONSHIP WITH
REASON   THE NOISE ASSOCIATED WITH A MOB IS THE ANTI-THESIS TO AN
ATMOSPHERE WHERE REASON IS POSSIBLE

SILENCE AND NOISE

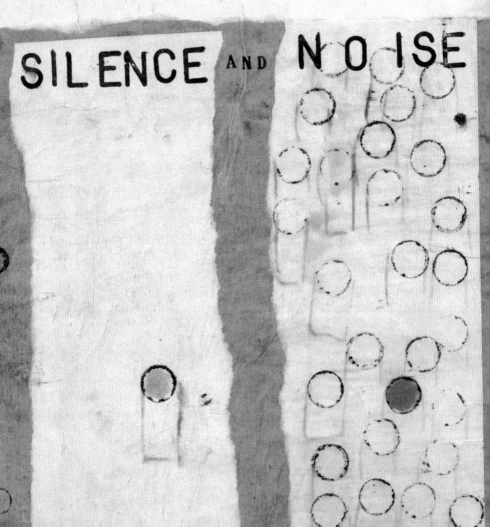

73

6

THE LOGBOOK
OF THE SHIP
"HENRY DAVID THOREAU"

AFGEGEVEN 4 APR. 1970

TWEEDE BOEK
THE THREE
KINGS
THEATER

SUMMARY, ACKNOWLEDGEMENT, AND EMPATHY

Now Sidsel summarizes what Philip has just told her.

SUMMARY

Sidsel
You are telling me that you are tired of not feeling OK and that you constantly seek acceptance of what you do. This is related to the fact that when you were a child, your mother constantly told you what to do. You are still subject to that pressure. You are sick and tired of it. For instance, you are tired of the fact that you need her acceptance of your tea project. If you are to die with that project, then you would want to die standing up.

Is it an OK summary?

Philip
Yes

ACKNOWLEDGEMENT

Sidsel
It makes good sense to me that you are sick and tired of constantly seeking acceptance of what you do. It also makes good sense that you reflect on your childhood, where this was also the case. Back then you also experienced that your mother constantly interfered. You are still influenced by that experience and I understand that – particularly now when you want to get started on the tea project. Have I understood you correctly?

Philip
Yes, you have understood quite a lot. I also said that if I should die with that project, then it should be with my dignity intact – standing up.

Sidsel
If you were to die with your tea project, it should be with your dignity intact.

EMPATHY

Sidsel
I imagine that you must feel angry, exasperated, and sad. Is that what you feel?

Philip
Yes, that is what I feel. I get sad and angry with my mother and with myself.

APPRECIATION

Sidsel
I appreciate that you invited me!

Philip
You appreciate that I invited you.

Sidsel
Yes, my confidence in you and the love I feel for you bring tears to my eyes right now.

Philip
The fact that you have confidence in me and love me brings tears to your eyes?

Philip sounds as if he is asking Sidsel a question. He realizes this and says:

Philip
Oops, that almost sounded like a question mark. I have too many of those in my life already. I will try again. It is your confidence in me and your love for me that bring tears to your eyes.

Sidsel
When you love me, I feel really loved.

Philip
When I love you, you feel really loved.

Philip continues with his appreciation:

I appreciate your presence. It feels so wonderful. When you are close, I feel really loved.

Sidsel
What you appreciate about me is my presence. When I am close, you feel really loved.

They fondle each other's hands. The atmosphere is peaceful, pure, warm, and loving. Again, Sidsel is obviously touched. Both take some deep breaths.

Oh, that feels good, Philip repeats. Gradually, they loosen their grips on each other, sit back in their chairs, and begin to reconnect with external reality.

TOO MUCH OF A GOOD THING IS WONDERFUL

– MAE WEST –

EATING THREE ELEPHANTS AT ONE TIME IS POSSIBLE IF THE ELEPHANTS
ARE SMALL E N O U G H AND IT IS ART TO MAKE SMALL ELEPHANTS AND ART

IS GOOD E A T I N G

AND COSTS NO ELEPHANTS
BUT ONLY SOME W O R K

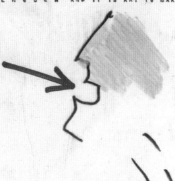

3 6. NOV. 1971

92

VEERTIENDE BOEK
THE
*B*I*G*
FOOL

NEW WAYS OF BEING

"But how often do I have to repeat this! I get so incredibly sad every time you scold the children in that way. When will you learn to control yourself?"

We recognize this situation *ad nauseam*. It is caused by a recurring frustration that results in a fight, which leaves us more at odds than the last time the situation surfaced.

Both partners are upset. One of the partners is distressed because of a sense of powerlessness stemming from not being able to get his or her point of view through to the other. The reason for the disappointment is also that it has not been possible to find a way to resolve the conflict. Hence, the situation repeats itself.

In this kind of situation it is helpful to consider the fact that frustrations can be understood as changes attempting to happen.

THE DIALOGUE OF ACKNOWLEDGEMENT AND CHANGE

The basic structure of the Dialogue of Acknowledgement can be expanded to include a section on change in order to focus on the wish for change that is manifesting itself. A focus on change is an extremely useful tool in dialogue, since it can transform conflict into new ways of being with one another.

The first half of the Dialogue of Acknowledgement and Change is the same as the dialogue that was described step by step on p. 168. After the first step, the dialogue now takes the couple on an exploration with the objective of discovering the roots of their frustrations. What does it look like, how does it feel, what does it mean, and where does it come from? Towards the end of the dialogue, the couple prepares a new plan of action which will address the longing of the partner expressing his or her frustration.

Taken as a whole, the Dialogue of Acknowledgement and Change are efficient because they give us the opportunity to find out what triggers our frustrations. It provides us with a window on to the strange mechanisms that, in no time at all, make us behave like wounded children who, for no apparent good reason, suddenly react uncontrollably.

The established framework of the dialogue creates the necessary space where we can be ourselves and be aware of each other. When we just criticize each other, we have no chance of changing. The more we criticize, the more we are confronted with our partner's undesirable survival strategies: anger, distancing, sarcasms, sulking, or resignation.

THE DUAL GIFT

Say yes! Every time you say yes to the Dialogue of Acknowledgement you begin to meet your partner's need for intimacy and change. You not only promote your partner's development, but also your own. The point is that you are also able to change the habits that have prevented you from achieving the desired connection with your partner.

Do not keep track of who contributes with the most invitations or changes. Let go of the over-scrupulous observance of democratic rights and debating procedures and the "quid pro quo" way of thinking once and for all. Consider every subject, every insight, and every suggestion of change a gift for each of you.

Remember that every change you make will fit with some of your partner's old experiences of not feeling cared for. So, every time you apply the dialogue to explore a frustration, there will be beneficial results for both of you – the dual gift!

The Dialogue of Acknowledgement and Change consists of the following steps:

1. PREPARATION
2. THE BRIDGE
3. APPRECIATION
4. CHOICE OF THEME
(1, 2, 3 and 4 are described on p. 168)

5. MY FRUSTRATION (MIRRORED BY THE LISTENER)
In relatively few sentences, the storyteller formulates what he or she finds frustrating about the listener's actions. Here, the type of

behaviour that *triggers* the frustration should be described. Do not speak about personality traits or blame the listener, or it will be difficult for the listener to remain within the large cogwheel.
The storyteller says:
I become frustrated when you . . .

6. MY FEELING (TO BE MIRRORED)
Immediately after the description of the frustration, the feelings are described.
The storyteller says:
. . . And when I experience that . . . (the frustration), *I get the feeling that . . . or then I begin to feel . . .*

7. MY IMPULSIVE REACTIONS (TO BE MIRRORED)
Here, the storyteller describes the ways in which he or she reacts: his or her survival strategies, my fight, flight, or freeze reaction – the small cogwheel. We have many ways to describe our familiar survival strategies.
The storyteller says:
. . . And what I do then is to . . . the way I respond is to . . .

8. MY PRESENT STORY (TO BE MIRRORED)
Here, the storyteller describes the deep meaning behind his or her emotional reaction. The storyteller says:
And when I react in that way, then my inner voice . . . or *At this point, I tell myself that . . .*

9. SUMMARY
The listener gives a short summary of the storyteller's frustration, the emotion described, the impulsive reaction, and the story-teller's message. He or she concludes with the words:
Did I get the most important issues? Or: *Was that an OK summary?*

10. ACKNOWLEDGMENT
The listener acknowledges the aspects of the storyteller's story. Again, the point is not to agree with the interpretation. The point is that we allow ourselves to see the world from our partner's perspective.

The listener could, for instance, begin by saying:
It makes good sense to me that . . .
I understand that you have experienced these issues in the way that you just told me.
Seeing these things with your eyes, I understand that . . .

If there is something that the listener has not understood, he or she could say:
I did not quite understand when you said . . .
Please help me to understand . . .

11. EMPATHY
The listener might, for instance, say:
I imagine that this has made you feel . . . (You should use only 2–3 words to describe that feeling.)

12. MY CHILDHOOD MEMORY (TO BE MIRRORED)
This requires that the storyteller connects with the feelings evoked by the childhood memory. The storyteller shares only one situation or a single image from the past or from his or her childhood. The storyteller says:
. . . these emotions remind me of . . .

13. MY GREATEST LONGING (TO BE MIRRORED)
Bearing the childhood memory in mind, what is it you longed for in your childhood and still long for today . . .?
The storyteller says:
I wish that I could always feel . . .

14. MY PRESENT WISH (TO BE MIRRORED)
This wish is more basic, concrete, and contemporary than the childhood longing.
The storyteller says:
Presently I would wish that you, for instance . . .

15. THREE WISHES FOR CHANGE ADDRESSED TO THE PARTNER (TO BE MIRRORED)
Here, the storyteller formulates three positive, measurable, and concrete wishes addressed to the partner/listener. The term positive is used because this is something that he or she wishes the partner to do, and not something the partner should stop

doing. If the storyteller formulates a negative wish, new criticism will ensue and the partners will end up in a deadlock.

The wishes should be measurable. That means there should be a very clear description of what is wished for. This enables the partner to know when he or she has successfully completed the task. The point here is not to make a promise "forever", but a promise to take one small step in the right direction.

Finally, the wishes must be *completely* concrete. The partner should not doubt what the storyteller wants. Here, we often experience how difficult it is to put into words what we want, as opposed to all the things we do not want.

The storyteller says:
. . . my first wish for change addressed to you is that . . . to be mirrored
. . . my second wish for change addressed to you is that . . . to be mirrored
. . . my third wish for change addressed to you is that . . . to be mirrored

The listener
Selects one of the wishes.
The listener should select a wish that he or she can honour and a wish which he or she finds challenging. The listener should not select a wish that he or she believes is the storyteller's preference. The storyteller thanks the listener for the gift.

16. CONCLUSION
The storyteller expresses what the gift means to him or her.
The storyteller says:
. . . In terms of my history and baggage the fact that you are willing to meet my wish means to me: . . .

The listener expresses:
What it means to him or her to give the gift.
. . . agreeing to meet your wish in this way and in relation to my personal history and baggage means to me: . . .

17. APPRECIATION
The entire dialogue is rounded off with a mutual appreciation about the experience of the dialogue. Both the storyteller and the listener take turns to speak.
I appreciate . . . about the way you have been present in this dialogue . . .

IT DOESN'T COME AUTOMATICALLY –
BUT IT IS WORTH EVERY MINUTE OF THE PROCESS

Our relationship has become a safer place to be for both of us. When the old anxiety-provoking conflicts recur, we use new patterns of response. We both show a much greater understanding of the other person's vulnerability, because we know and understand it better.

This understanding influences the shared space we create, and it becomes safer, but only because we work on it. It does not happen automatically. It requires our constant attention and motivation to observe the patterns which each one of us carries with us in our backpacks, and which cause us to clash repeatedly in the same conflicts. Previously small issues quickly escalated, because we were unaware of what was going on.

One of the things we tend to avoid now is, for instance, criticizing and blaming each other. When it occasionally happens, we do not go all the way, you could say. It is easier to forgive the other person's annoying behaviours when we understand why they annoy us, what they remind us of, and what our own share of the annoyances and frustrations is all about.

The safe space between us, to apply a term used in the Dialogue of Acknowledgement, is important to us. These days we make an effort to improve the space by acknowledgement and listening.

Of course, we are still occasionally frustrated and annoyed. Now and then we also tell each other about issues that frustrate us. However, we always find an appropriate time and place to do so. You could say that both of us hold back more.

We have both become better at understanding the significance of listening to what the other person is telling us. We are also better at restraining ourselves, so that we do not dump all our problems on our partner. It is quite demanding to listen to frustrations.

Personally, we feel that we develop together as well as individually. To me, Tone, the Dialogue of Acknowledgement has meant a lot. The insights are drawn out one by one and I gradually get more in touch with my authentic self – the part of me which lives in the shadow.

For a person with my history, it is amazing to experience mirroring and empathic acknowledgement. It makes me blossom and my self-confidence increases. This is, however, an "exercise" which should be practised, and, little by little, I am integrating the process on deeper levels.

As far as I, Christian, am concerned, my experience is similar to Tone's. From my perspective, the main point is that I have gained more insight into myself and a greater understanding and consciousness of the patterns in my history. I am now aware of how my personal history causes problems in my life and in my relationship. Recently, this has resulted in the fact that I have stopped smoking after forty years of using cigarettes to curb my anxiety. The dialogues enabled me to make the connection with issues in my childhood that stress reminds me of. That knowledge has helped me to stop smoking completely for the first time in my life. Apparently, I do not need to light up a cigarette. That is wonderful!

It is very simple – but the most simple things are often the most difficult to practise. For this reason, therapy guided by a therapist for couples also means a lot to us. In this field our therapists have also functioned as good, mature role models. However, we should not fool ourselves. Change does not come automatically, and the road is paved with blood, sweat, and tears. But it is worth every minute.

Tone and Christian

TONE AND CHRISTIAN

Christian and Tone have known each other for twelve years and have two children. For three years they have used the Dialogue of Acknowledgement on both personal and professional levels. In this dialogue, the theme is the insecurity and anxiety Tone feels when Christian behaves in a particular way. Little by little, the insecurity and anxiety are unravelled, allowing the underlying story to surface.

PREPARATION

Christian and Tone position themselves on two chairs. Christian's knees are touching Tone's knees.

The palms of their hands are open and rest on their thighs. Christian and Tone sit for a while in this position in order to become grounded and sense what it is like to be present in the moment here and now.

THE BRIDGE

Now Tone and Christian go on a mental journey from their own place into the mutual space, into the shared energy that is the bond between them. For a while they explore what it is like to be in that space.

Then they begin by offering appreciations to each other. Christian says that he would like to go first.

APPRECIATION

Christian
Lately, I have been thinking that one of the things I really appreciate about you is that you are capable of containing my big feelings. For instance, when I shout a little too much you do not allow that to frighten you. To me, that means that I am able to return to myself without feeling that I have done something completely wrong.

Tone mirrors
You appreciate the fact that when you get angry and happen to shout a little too much, then I am able to contain you without getting frightened. That means that you can return to yourself quickly. Did I remember everything?

Christian
Yes, you did.

Tone appreciates
I really appreciate your good moods and the glint in your eyes.

Christian mirrors
You appreciate the glint in my eyes and my good moods.

Tone
The fact that you focus on the positive aspects gives me a profound confidence that everything will work out well. That also means that my belief in the future is strengthened.

Christian
Because I focus on the positive aspects and have a profound belief that everything will be all right, you also believe in the future.

CHOICE OF THEME AND OF STORYTELLER AND LISTENER ROLES

Tone
My theme has to do with boundaries. It is difficult for me when your boundaries are unclear.

Christian
You find it difficult when my boundaries are unclear.
My theme concerns abandonment. I am terrified of being abandoned and of being alone. And I wonder if I am good enough and all right as a person.

Tone
Your theme is that you occasionally are afraid of being abandoned because you are not good enough. Is there more?

Christian
Yes, it invades my mind in all kinds of ways.
I find it interesting that you feel this way about my boundaries. I would like to hear more about that.

Tone
I had the impression I should be the one to listen. Last time it was also me who did the talking.

Christian
I had completely forgotten, but I would really like to hear more about how you see my boundaries. I also need to practise listening and mirroring.

Tone
Then let us do that.

PRESENTATION OF THE FRUSTRATION

Christian
Tone, I would really like to hear something about your difficulties with my unclear boundaries. I will visit you and I am really curious about what you want to tell me. (The bridge).

Tone
I have been thinking about a kind of tension I feel when you are around. Sometimes it has a positive and sometimes a negative effect on me.

Christian
You are saying that you feel a tension when we are together and that it has both positive and negative aspects.

MY FEELINGS

Tone
Even if, in many ways, I am a calm and balanced person, there are times with you when I feel a physical tension and restless-ness. When I have that feeling, I experience that I take control and want to manage everything.

Christian
Even if you are a calm and balanced person, there are occasion-ally times when you feel tense. Especially when our vibrations clash. In that situation you want to control and take the lead. Was that what you said?

Tone
No, I do not want to take control in that way. I actually do not like that. I think I do it because I am trying to get rid of the tension and the unrest.

Christian
Then you take control, even if you do not like it. You think this may be because you attempt to get rid of the tension in that way.

MY IMPULSIVE BEHAVIOUR

Tone
It is difficult for me when you respond in unpredictable ways. For instance, when you feel you should solve the problems for me or when you get angry if I try to control and take charge.

Christian
You get many kinds of reactions from me. For instance, when I would like to solve the problems for you or when I get angry.

Tone
It is strange that I should come to a halt at this point. It is as if I cannot think of an example of your reactions that trigger these tensions . . .

Time passes . . .

Christian, it is difficult for me when, for instance, you get angry. Then I try to remain calm by creating distance between us.

Christian
You are saying that you protect yourself by distancing yourself when I get angry. Did I get what you said?

Tone
Yes, then I get a little uptight. I distance myself because I get so annoyed when I cannot feel in which direction you are going. When you skip from one thing to the next. For instance, you think that we should just have a cup of tea or a glass of red wine when we are about to go to bed and have to get up early. I get really annoyed when your boundaries change like that. They are all over the place terms of red wine, work, bedtime, and food.

Christian
*You get more severe, distance yourself and become annoyed . . .
no, I cannot remember what you said. Would you please repeat?*

Tone
*Yes, I do not like it when I cannot sense what you want to do,
when you skip from one thing to the next. First you say we should
have a cup of tea, and then you say we should have a glass of red
wine, even if it is late and we have to get up early. This happens
with many issues: red wine, bedtimes, and the time we spend
with the children.*

Christian
*You do not like it when you cannot sense what I want. When I
skip from one thing to the next. You are thinking, for instance, of
red wine, food, bedtimes, and when I spend time with the
children. Did I get everything?*

Tone
Yes, you did.

MY PRESENT STORY

Tone
*I have a problem with the fact that I cannot be clear about your
boundaries. Actually, right now I feel very angry when I see that
you cannot set boundaries for your behaviour. The reason for
my anger is that your problem with boundaries has an impact
on our lives. I feel that we are missing out on various things and
wasting our time.*

Christian
*You have a problem with the fact that you cannot be clear about
my boundaries. Right now this actually makes you feel angry.
You think we waste time because of this issue.*

SUMMARY, ACKNOWLEDGEMENT, AND EMPATHY

Christian now gives a short summary of Tone's frustrations and
moves into acknowledgement and empathy.

Christian
It makes very good sense to me that you attempt to deal with your restlessness by becoming a "control mama". It also makes sense that it can be difficult to watch me skip from one thing to the next without knowing what I want. Do you feel that I have understood you?

Tone
Yes

EMPATHY

Christian
I think that you must be annoyed and feel confused and angry. Is that correct?

Tone
Yes, I feel apprehensive, angry, and also insecure.

Christian
You become apprehensive, angry, and insecure. Is that correct? Are there any other emotions?

Tone
No.

MY CHILDHOOD MEMORY

What does all this remind you of? Here the focus is: where do these feelings come from – which early memories do they call forth or match?

Tone
I believe this reminds me of my mother's lack of boundaries. Her life was a mess and without goals and direction. When she was on a binge, I withdrew into myself in order to be able to survive.

My impression is that I remember the tension and restlessness around the ages 8–10. The feeling that surfaces is that I felt useless and insecure.

Christian
You are telling me that you were around 8–10 years old when

you first remembered the feeling of this tension. You felt useless. Is there more?

Tone
I did not know what the truth was and what were lies. Is she or is she not drinking again? Is she there or isn't she?

Christian
You did not know what was true, whether she drank or not, and whether she was or wasn't there.

Tone
I believe that what hurt me the most was that my mother was not in touch with me. I could not reach her and everything was complete chaos.

Christian
What hurt you the most was that your mother did not have contact with you and that everything was a complete chaos.

MY GREATEST LONGING

Tone
My greatest longing was that she would pull herself together and gather all the different characters she embodied into one strong person with whom I could feel secure and whom I knew for a fact could take good care of me.

Christian
You wish she had pulled herself together and had become a complete person who could make you feel secure, and who could take care of you. Have I understood you correctly?

Tone is touched, the tears are rolling down her cheeks, while she nods and continues to tell her story.

Tone
I remember that as a very lonely time filled with anxiety. That is what I remember best. Being alone and frightened.

Christian
You remember that time as lonely and full of anxiety.

Tone
They were not in control of anything. Now and then everything was OK. It was as if they pulled themselves together. But after a week or two they were all at sea again.

Tone takes a long break and Christian does not interrupt the silence. Tone continues:

I think it was at this point that I learnt to protect myself by distancing myself so that I would not constantly be drawn into that circus.

Christian
You say that they were not in control of anything. Occasionally, it was OK, but when they began drinking, they were all at sea again. In order to protect yourself against this circus, you learnt to distance yourself.

Tone
Nobody worried about me or noticed how alone and frightened I felt. I longed for a calm, predictable situation.

Christian
Nobody worried about you or saw how frightened you were. You longed for a quiet and predictable life. Is there more?

Tone is still very affected by these memories. She rests a little, recovers, and shakes her head.

Tone
No, that was precisely what it was like, she says.

MY PRESENT WISH

Tone
One of the things I realized while telling you about this is that I long to see you take better care of yourself. I want you to be completely intact.

Christian
You have realized that you long for me to take better care of myself . . . so that I remain intact. Have I heard you?

Tone
Yes, because when I know that you can take better care of yourself, then I can relax more, and be more at ease. Then I will not have to control and manage as much in our shared space in order to take care of myself.

Christian
Yes, because if I could take better care of myself, then you could relax more and stop controlling so much.

MY WISHES FOR CHANGE

After some time, Tone says:

I wish that you would only drink red wine during the weekends and that you tell me when you have made a decision about this. You should also make up your own mind about the time frame for this.

Christian
Your first wish is that I only drink red wine during weekends and that I myself tell you about the timeframe in which I decide to do that.

Tone
My second wish is that you limit the time in which your mobile phone is on. I wish you would set a limit as to how much you want to be disturbed by your mobile phone and that you tell me about your decision and the timeframe you have selected.

Christian
Your second wish is that I limit the time during which my mobile phone is on and that I myself decide how long that timeframe should be.

Christian does not need a lot of time to consider this.

Christian
I have no problems with any of these wishes. In fact, both would be good for me. However, I choose to only drink red wine at our evening meals during the weekends for the next two months.

CONCLUSION, THE DUAL GIFT: THANK YOU!

Tone
It means so much to me, Christian, that you really observe and reflect on what truly matters in your life. Even if it doesn't seem like much, it actually means a great deal for me to be confident that you are capable of establishing some healthy boundaries in your life. Nor do you have any idea how much it moves me that you know about my vulnerability – my chaotic childhood. I believe that with these agreements in mind, I can become a lot wiser in terms of understanding the old tension and restlessness in my baggage.

Christian
To me, this means that when I go to bed with you at 11 p.m., instead of drinking a couple of glasses of red wine and spending an hour or two in front of the computer or the television, I will no longer feel like a stupid caveman.

It feels a little like making things safer because I am concerned about my own, but also your well-being, Tone. I now realize how many negative emotions are triggered when my boundaries are unclear. I must be more clear. By the way, having said that, I feel my own resistance to going ahead with this. It is as if my mother suddenly interferes, warning and admonishing me to do all kinds of things because they would be good for me. I now realize this will take more energy than I anticipated and that I must make an effort.

Tone
I fully realize that. Incidentally, I am surprised that you managed to guide me through all these rooms. I had not imagined that that would have been possible. I just began by exploring a feeling, and then we ended up here. That is amazing. Actually, we have had quite a number of conflicts about this issue. Because I felt secure, I had no problem committing to this process. Even if it meant dealing with some very painful issues, it felt good doing it with you. Thank you for that.

THE DIALOGUE OF ACKNOWLEDGEMENT WITH CHANGE

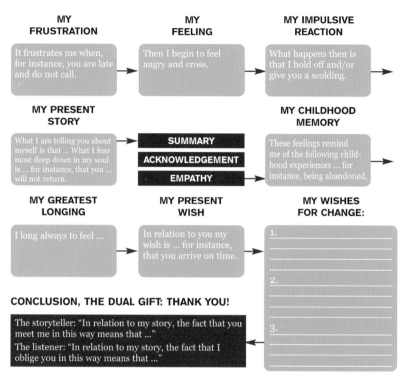

MY FRUSTRATION

It frustrates me when, for instance, you are late and do not call.

MY FEELING

Then I begin to feel angry and cross.

MY IMPULSIVE REACTION

What happens then is that I hold off and/or give you a scolding.

MY PRESENT STORY

What I am telling you about myself is that ... What I fear most deep down in my soul is ... for instance, that you ... will not return.

SUMMARY
ACKNOWLEDGEMENT
EMPATHY

MY CHILDHOOD MEMORY

These feelings remind me of the following childhood experiences ... for instance, being abandoned.

MY GREATEST LONGING

I long always to feel ...

MY PRESENT WISH

In relation to you my wish is ... for instance, that you arrive on time.

MY WISHES FOR CHANGE:

1.

2.

3.

CONCLUSION, THE DUAL GIFT: THANK YOU!

The storyteller: "In relation to my story, the fact that you meet me in this way means that ..."
The listener: "In relation to my story, the fact that I oblige you in this way means that ..."

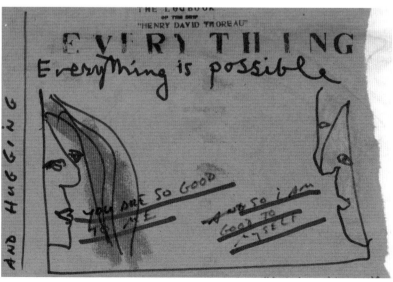

DRINK WATER

SEPTEMBER 26, 1970

THE LOGBOOK
OF THE BRIG
"HENRY DAVID THOREAU"

NEW STEPS –
FOR THE REST OF OUR LIVES

A bove and beyond the Dialogue of Acknowledgement and the way of thinking we have introduced in this book, we also need special "vitamins" such as pleasure and enjoyment. These vitamins will help our love stay on track and develop. Enjoyment helps us to keep our defences down. When we are enjoying life with our loved one, we enable our "small cogwheel" (the fight, flight, and freeze brain) to start believing that our partner is not "dangerous". Then, all our survival strategies can be abandoned because the relationship feels safe and sound.

Moreover, we should constantly be open to affirming the resources which are already present in the relationship. If we need to break some vicious circle of behaviour, we will need to access all that we know works well in the relationship that we love and cherish. We can do this by using the Dialogue of Acknowledgement, using exercises and daily reminders, and by creating a shared vision of the life we would like to live.

The new steps could be the exercises described on the following pages:

- – Ten daily opportunities for development.
- – Back to nurture.
- – Surprises.
- – The pursuit of happiness.
- – Be aware of the transitions.
- – The shared vision.
- – Ideas for other dialogues.

This catalogue can be viewed as a series of suggestions and opportunities. The way people respond to such exercises varies. Some are delighted and find them beneficial. Others would rather design their own experiments. We hope these exercises will be a source of inspiration and enjoyment to you.

EXERCISE 8

–

TEN DAILY OPPORTUNITIES FOR DEVELOPMENT

We are each other's touchstones of growth and development. We are, so to speak, each other's sculptors. The following ten-point catalogue describes some daily opportunities for growth.

1. Dialogue, dialogue, dialogue.

2. Replace criticism, aggression, guilt and shame with a request for dialogue.

3. We should appreciate our partner on a daily basis. Perhaps it will be beneficial to do it at a certain time, for instance at breakfast, or when we have gone to bed.

4. In the heat of the moment, when our reactions are stronger than we like, we could take private time out to consider the extent to which our reaction belongs to our story and our past and the extent to which it is purely a response to the present situation.

5. Create security by emphasizing the positive things in our lives. Through doing this, there will be more of an overall positive focus in our lives.

6. Consider ways and means of investing in our shared space.

7. Observe the inner child as well as the adult in our partner and understand that both have unfulfilled longings.

8. Everyone has a right to a personal vision of the world. Acknowledge our differences instead of allowing them to escalate into a power struggle.

9. Consider the fact that the frustrations that our partner provokes in us may be based on unfulfilled longings from our childhood.

10. Instead of criticizing, we should focus on saying what we want.

EXERCISE 9

–

BACK TO NURTURE

Once we were very good at taking care of each other. We took time for small gestures expressing gratitude, affection, and consideration. This exercise focuses on increasing our awareness of nurture. In short, we should allow ourselves the opportunity to vary our patterns of behaviour, to become more caring and nurturing than we are at the moment. It might be a good idea to write down our thoughts separately before we mirror each other.

1. Finish the following sentence in as many ways you can. Be specific, concrete, and positive.

I feel that you care/that I am loved by you, when you . . .

2. Recall the time when you were in love with your partner. Complete the sentence below describing the ways in which your partner used to be caring and considerate in ways that made you feel loved. Be concrete, specific, describing positively and quantitatively (how much and how often).

I felt that you cared for me/that I was loved by you when you . . .

3. There might be some nurturing and loving actions that you have always longed for, but never asked for. They might be hidden and secret wishes you have never voiced before. Not everyone has such wishes but quite a few of us have. The reason is that we often have the quite erroneous idea that if our partner really loves us, then he or she would intuitively fulfil our secret wishes.

However, this idea is not realistic. In real life, we need to let our partner know our longings and wishes. Otherwise our partner will never know. He or she is not a mind reader.

We could begin this exercise by saying, for instance, "I would like to tell you about some secret and deep wishes of mine. In so doing, I am willing to put aside my fear of . . . I wish that . . .

4. Share your lists by taking one item at a time, and, in turn, you and your partner read the wishes out loud, while the one not reading mirrors.

EXERCISE 10

–

BE AWARE OF THE TRANSITIONS

On any given day there will be times that are particularly important to our sense of mutual connection. Focus on the following transitions that occur every single day. It is beneficial to be aware of the quality of the connection between us during transitions.

1. The first thing we do when we wake up in the morning. What "message" do we send to our partner?

2. When one of us leaves the house. How do we say goodbye?

3. When we get home. How do we say hello?

4. When we go to sleep. Do we have some concluding loving messages for our partner just before he or she goes to sleep?

EXERCISE 11

–

SURPRISES

Surprises are a wonderful way of bringing new energy into the relationship. Just think of how wonderful it is for us to surprise young children and how thrilled they are. The same goes for adults – particularly when they are surprised with a gift of something they have wished for.

1. Make a list of surprises that you know would please your partner. The list should be based on your memory of previous successful surprises, wishes expressed, or casual remarks your partner has made about his or her special longings.

You should not shock your partner with a surprise that you *think* he or she would like.

2. Save the list and make good use of it from time to time.

3. It doesn't have to be surprises in the a-trip-to-Rome category every time. Much less will do. For instance, breakfast in bed.

In our own relationship, such a surprise breakfast in bed developed into a recurring morning ritual that has become very special to us. Here, we discuss the world situation – and sometimes much more – over a cup of tea before we get up.

EXERCISE 12

–

PLEASURE

Some of the most joyful experiences occur when we have fun together. At that particular moment we feel that we have a special connection. However, unfortunately, it is often much easier for us to contact the wounded child inside us than the playful child.

For this reason we have to invite and tease out the playful child. Playing is good for us. Like orgasm, the deep laughter produces high levels of endorphins, the body's pleasure and happiness hormone. This is where we achieve the most effective calming of our ancient "fight, flight, and freeze" dominated brain.

1. Make a list of pleasurable and fun things – physically powerful and emotionally intense activities, which you would like to do with your partner. It might be fun to dance the tango, throw a big party once a year, watch an entertaining play or a film, sleep out, play games, go for a spontaneous city break and spend the night in a hotel, or drive to the seaside and go for a long walk on the beach.

2. Share your list with your partner, who will, in turn, mirror your suggestions for pleasure. Select one or two suggestions from each list and carry them out within the next month.

–

DIALOGUES ABOUT THE HISTORY AND PHILOSOPHY OF OUR RELATIONSHIP

Below you will find eleven suggestions for dialogues about your relationship. You should experiment with them one at a time when you have the energy and feel motivated and curious. One of you should tell his or her story while the other listens and mirrors.

THE HISTORY OF OUR RELATIONSHIP

DIALOGUE 1
About how we met and fell in love. What was it about our partner that made him or her special? What was our first impression of each other?

DIALOGUE 2
About our states of mind when we began dating. What aspects do we remember in particular? How long did we know each other prior to our dating? What were some of the major events? What conflicts did we have? What did we do together?

DIALOGUE 3
How did we decide to live together? How did we make up our mind that of all the people in the world, we wanted to live with him or her?

DIALOGUE 4
About the time when we first began living together. What was easy and good? Was there anything we had to get used to?

DIALOGUE 5
About the transition into parenthood. What was that time like?

DIALOGUE 6
About our entire relationship. When we look back, what moments or times stand out as particularly happy? What does it mean to us to "be happy as a couple"?

DIALOGUE 7
Ups and downs. Many relationships have ups and downs. Does that also apply to our relationship? Talk about some of these ups and downs.

DIALOGUE 8
About the difficult times in our relationship. What stands out as really difficult times? Why did we stay together despite such times? How did we get through these difficult times?

DIALOGUE 9
About the things we used to do together and which used to make us happy.

OUR RELATIONSHIP PHILOSOPHY

DIALOGUE 10
Which factors constitute a good relationship? Which of the couples you know do you think have particularly good relationships and which couples do you think have particularly bad relationships? What is the difference? How would you compare them with your relationship?

DIALOGUE 11
About our parents' relationships. Does your relationship resemble their relationships, or are they completely different?

Source: Developed from Gottman (1999).

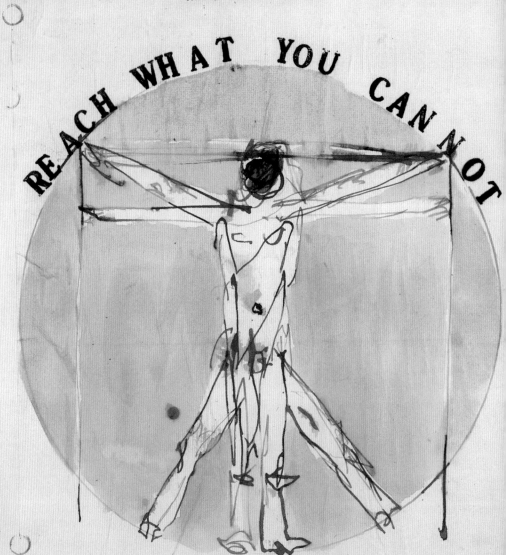

thank you LEONARDO

THE LOGBOOK
OF THE SHIP
"HENRY DAVID THOREAU"

REACH WHAT YOU CANNOT

9 JULI 1971   17⁴⁰   9 JULI 1971   17⁴⁰   9 JULI 1971   17⁴⁰   9 JULI 1971   17⁴⁰

88

OUR LIFE TOGETHER

Most of the work in this book is based on events in the past. In the final chapter, we will attempt to create closure by addressing the future on the basis of the present.

It is incredibly inspiring and motivating to work towards a goal. We might call it a vision: a vision of what our dream relationship could be like in five, ten, or twenty years!

Much scientific research confirms that the distinguishing characteristic of stable couples and families who function well is a clear vision of what they can do together. That means that they have clear goals and visions for their shared lives.

As couples, we have a choice. We can allow ourselves to be driven more or less randomly by a past that we did not choose, or we can direct ourselves towards a future that we choose to design.

From the world of sport, we are familiar with the results of working with visualizations. Having clear goals and visions makes a colossal difference both in terms of training and performance. Visualizations are a natural extension of this process.

Visualizations mean that, in a state of complete calm, we imagine what it feels like to achieve – to be in our visions. We imagine, for instance, what it feels like to slide across the goal-line as a winner, or, with our inner eye, we see our own power and strength.

We can transfer this knowledge directly to our relationship. By describing our visions in concrete ways, we can start a conscious process that will lead us to our goals. Many small decisions will lead us to a shared vision that we have created with our own words.

LEARNING IN REVERSE

"I first became aware of the power of visualization when I was around 13–14 years old and had decided to learn to ride backwards on my bike. At that age you do things like that . . .

I practised untiringly, but could not learn to do it. In fact, I gave up. However, unconsciously, I had not quite given up. A month later I tried again.

Bliss! I was riding backwards on my bike! Victory. I could do it!!

I had not trained in the least and it was quite simply a revelation to discover that the ability existed somewhere in my system – I have no idea where. I had, quite simply, clung to the idea that I wanted to learn it. Because of this visualization I had been able to work on it unconsciously.

Piet

WHAT IS THE MOST BEAUTIFUL AND THE NOBLEST THING?
IT IS JUST TO WISH FOR A QUIET AND HARMONIOUS MIND,
TO PLANT A TREE IN THE YARD AND A FLOWER IN THE POT.
THE REPOSE BECOMES PERFECT
WHEN APPRECIATED WITH WINE OR TEA,
OR WHEN IN THE COMPANY OF INTIMATE FRIENDS
WE EXPRESS SINCERE EMOTIONS.
OTHER THINGS WE IGNORE OR DISMISS.
IF YOU DO NOT PAY ATTENTION TO UNIMPORTANT THINGS,
THEN YOUR JOY WILL BE UNPRECEDENTED.

– INSCRIPTION ON PIET'S CHINESE WATER PIPE –

EXERCISE 14

–

OUR VISION

Which dream images appear on the screen of our minds when we think about our future? Where are we, what does it look like, what are we doing, how do we feel, how do we live, and what matters most?

1. What are our wildest dreams of the future? Describe them positively, and in the present tense, one, three, and five years into the future. Make a list.

2. Share the list with your partner, who then mirrors.

3. Your partner then shares his or her list and you mirror.

4. Together, make a list of your shared dreams and visions and put it on the fridge.

THE BEST VERSION OF OURSELVES

The acknowledging space has been a must for a break-through in my life. Without the Dialogue of Acknowledge-ment I would not have been able to lean back confidently with an open mind in relation to myself and to Flemming. In that atmosphere, you become the best version of yourself and you become present in a different way. In this space, I suddenly think that my partner looks different: more beautiful and gentle . . . so that anything can happen.

When we rest in each other's acknowledging gaze for a suffi-cient amount of time, I realize what it is most important for me to say right now. Then the sentence comes to me: "You can count on me." This sentence becomes important because it is and always was a recurring theme in my life, as well as in our shared life.

Our history has been told many times in the Dialogue of Acknowledgement, and it will be told again. Even though it is painful, my experience is one of understanding – a com-plete mutual understanding of something important. This is where we reach the melting point between the two of us. It may happen during a process of acknowledgement, or when I mirror Flemming. Suddenly, I sense that he really under-stands how to travel with me on the journey through life. We go the same places, but we see something new every time.

Getting to the melting point is hard work. It is not always a logical process. However, the reward is wonderful, because then we are completely united. At that point, there is nothing under the sun that is too difficult to talk about. At that point, he understands everything.

Ulla

– Ulla and Flemming have been married for forty years. During the past five years they have applied the Dialogue of Acknowledgement on personal and professional levels.

Use the dialogue and the acknowledgement to find and develop the love in your vibrant relationship. Good luck!

Giving
Controlling
Quick
Rude
Flexible
Cheerful
Critical
Economical
Resolute
Untruthful
Shy
Tense
Immature
Devoted
Kind
Brave
Virtuous
Creative
Responsible
Respectful
Reliable
Brutal
Foolish
Affectionate
Humble
Violent

Jealous
Hasty
Courageous
Offensive
Insensitive
Aggressive
Spiritual
Trustworthy
Tight-fisted
Sincere
Forthcoming
Allied
Open
Particular
Insistent
Cold
Impatient
Clever
Amusing
Pleasant
Considerate
Capricious
Nervous
Acknowledging
Accessible

Honest
Careful
Frightened
Observant
Loving
Supportive
Closed
Confident
Fair
Arrogant
Rigid
Engaged
Honourable
Cunning
Objective
Loyal
Tolerant
Disinterested
Sensitive
Amiable
Tedious
Serious
Hard
Fragile
Listening

EMOTIONAL WORDS

Positive	Positive	Negative	Negative
Vibrant	Brave	Hopeless	Guilty
Happy	Important	Powerless	Lonely
Satisfied	Optimistic	Tired	Isolated
In love	Jolly	Despairing	Abandoned
Energetic	Enthusiastic	Angry	Betrayed
Relieved	Trusting	Furious	Deceived
Certain	Self-assured	Sad	Deserted
Fortunate	Outspoken	Unhappy	Misunderstood
Calm	Strong	Distressed	Overlooked
Serene	Determined	Inconsolable	Ignored
Carefree	Loving	Spiteful	Boring
Sexy	Curious	Shameful	Frightened
Satiated	Proud	Ridiculous	Rejected
Relaxed	Delighted	Hurt	Inadequate
Warm	Dependent	Incompetent	Depressed
Cold			Independent

REFERENCES AND BIBLIOGRAPHY

INTRODUCTION
Hendrix, H., & LaKelly Hunt, H. (2004). *Receiving Love*. New York: Atria.
Rogers, C. (1951). *Client Centered Therapy*. London: Constable & Robinson.
Rogers, C. (1961). *On Becoming a Person – a Therapist's View of Psychotherapy*. London: Constable & Robinson.

WHY DO WE GET LOST IN LOVE?
Buber, M. (1997). *I and Thou*. New York.
Casemore, R. (2006). *Person-centred Counselling in a Nutshell*. London: Sage.
Goleman, D. (2006). Social Intelligence. *New York: Random House.*
Gottman, J. M. (1999). *The Seven Principles for Making Marriage Work*. New York: Crown.
Hendrix, H., & LaKelly Hunt, H. (2004). *Receiving Love*. New York: Atria.
Honneth, A. (1996). *The Struggle for Recognition*.
Lynge, B. (2007). *Anerkendende Pædagogik*. Copenhagen: Dansk Psykologisk Forlag.
Love, P.†(2001). *The Truth about Love*. New York: Fireside.
McNamee, S., & Gergen, K. J. (1999). *Relational Responsibility*. New York: Sage.
Morgan, A. (2000). *What Is Narrative Therapy?* Melbourne: Gecko.
Rholes, S. W., & Simpson, J. A. (2004). *Adult Attachment*. New York: Guilford Press.
Rogers, C. (1961). *On Becoming a Person – A Therapist's View of Psychotherapy*. London: Constable & Robinson.
Simon, J. S. (2005). *Imago – Kærlighedens Terapi*. København, Dansk Psykologisk Forlag.
Stern, D. J. (1997). *The Motherhood Constellation*. New York: Basic Books.

WHAT ARE YOU CARRYING IN YOUR BAGGAGE?
Hendrix, H. (1988). *Getting the Love You Want: a Guide for Couples*. New York: Henry Holt.

THE ABILITY TO LOVE IS FORMED DURING INFANCY
Fonagy, P. (2001). *Attachment Theory and Psychoanalysis*. London: Karnac.
Holmes, J. (2001). *A Search for the Secure Base – Attachment Theory and Psychotherapy*. Hove: Routledge.
Gullestrup, L. (2005). *At blive et med sig selv – om udviklingen af det 0-5-Årige barns Selv*. København: Frydenlund.
Hendrix, H., & Lakelly Hunt, H. (1997). *Giving the Love that Heals – a Guide for Parents*. New York: Pocket Books.
Mortensen, K. V. (2001). *Fra Neuroser til Relationsforstyrrelser*. København: Gyldendal.
Schibbye, A. Løvlie (2005). *Relationer – et Dialektisk Perspektiv*. København: Akademisk forlag.
Seidenfaden, K., & Simon, J. (2003). *Couples Weekend Manual*. Inspired by, and translated from, Harville Hendrix, PhD (1979, revised December 1999) *Getting the Love You Want. Workshop Manual*.
Siegel, D. (2007). *The Mindful Brain*. New York: Norton.

Siegel, D. J., & Hartzell, M. (2003). *Parenting from the Inside Out*. New York: Penguin Putnam.
Smith, L. (2003). *Tilknytning og Børns Udvikling*. København: Akademisk Forlag.
Stern, D. J. (1997). *The Motherhood Constellation*. New York: Basic Books.
Stern, D. J. (1985). *The Interpersonal World of the Infant*. New York: Basic Books.

YOUR BRAIN IS A PARTNER AS WELL AS AN OPPONENT
Allen, J. G. & Fonagy, P. (Eds.) (2006). *Handbook of Mentalization-Based Treatment*. Chichester: Wiley.
Cozolino, L. (2006). *The Neuroscience of Human Relationships*. New York: Norton.
Damasio, A. (2000). *The Feelings of What Happens – Body, Emotion, and the Making of Consciousness*. New York: Vintage.
Fonagy, P. (2002). *Affect Regulation, Mentalization and the Development of the Self*. London: Other Press.
Hart, S. (2006). *Betydningen af Samhørighed – om Neuroaffektiv Udviklingspsykologi*. København: Reitzel.
LeDoux, J. (1998). *The Emotional Brain*. New York: Phoenix.
LeDoux, J. (2002). *Synaptic self – How Our Brains Become Who We Are*. New York: Viking Penguin.
Lewis, T., Lannon, R. & Amini, F. (2000). *A General Theory of Love*. New York: Vintage.
Siegel, D. J. (1999). *The Developing Mind*. New York: Guilford Press.
Siegel, D. J. (2007). *The Mindful Brain*. New York: Norton.

HOW ABOUT TONIGHT, DARLING?
Love, P. (2001). *The Truth about Love*. New York: Fireside.
Love, P., & Stosny, S. (2007). *How to Improve Your Marriage without Talking About It*. New York: Broadway Books.

PATHWAYS TO THE VIBRANT RELATIONSHIP
Cooperider, C. F. (2001). *Appreciative Inquiry: an Emerging Direction for Organization Development*. New York: Stipes.
Gottman, J. M. (1999). The Seven Principles for Making Marriage Work. *New York: Crown.*
Voetman, K., Dalsgaard, C., & Meisner, T. (2002). *Værdsat – Værdsættende Samtale i Praksis*. København: Psykologisk forlag.
Voetman, K., Dalsgaard, C. & Meisner, T. (2003). *Forvandling – Værdsættende Samtale i Teori og Praksis*. København: Psykologisk Forlag.

BEFORE THE DIALOGUE OF ACKNOWLEDGEMENT
Hendrix, H., & Lakelly Hunt, H. (2004). *Receiving Love*. New York: Atria.
Stern, D. J. (1985). *The Interpersonal World of the Infant*. New York: Basic Books.

NEW STEPS – FOR THE REST OF OUR LIVES
Hendrix, H. (1988). *Getting the Love You Want: a Guide for Couples*. New York: Henry Holt.

THE RELATIONSHIP THERAPY CENTRE
Seidenfaden and Draiby

Imago Relationship Therapy was first introduced in Denmark in 1998, when the Danish Imago Institute was founded. In 2003 Kirsten Seidenfaden and Piet Draiby continued the momentum by giving workshops and providing clinical training for therapists at the Relationship Therapy Centre. The Centre offers therapy designed for couples on the basis of the Dialogue of Acknowledgement and Relationship Therapy, as well as weekend seminars. Since the foundation of the centre, more than 1000 couples have participated in these seminars.

In addition, the Centre has established a post-qualifying two-year training programme for therapists. Since 2005, more than seventy people have participated in this training programme at the Centre for Relationship Therapy and are currently working as relationship therapists with couples in Denmark.

The new post-qualifying training programme has been accredited since 2003, by The Danish Psychological Association and The Danish Psychiatric Society. The Centre has also hosted a number of shorter and longer introductory courses, as well as introductory lectures for professionals.

Moreover, the Centre has in recent years offered a number of courses in peer group supervision within municipal and county districts. The Centre also offers training and coaching for individuals and groups of professionals in public and private sector organizations.

The Centre's administrative office and clinic are located in Christianshavn, Copenhagen, and it also runs a clinic in Svendborg.

CENTRE FOR RELATION FOCUSED THERAPY

Administration, Consultation and Training
Overgaden Neden Vandet 33 st.
1414 København K
Denmark
Tel: 0045 62 591946
Email: post@relationsterapi.dk
www.relationsterapi.dk

POSTSCRIPT AND ACKNOWLEDGEMENTS

Our heartfelt thanks to Mette Marie Davidsen for being the driving force behind this project, for her energy, courage, expertise, and for being willing to take a chance on us. Ever generous, she has shared these wonderful traits with us in an instructive, reciprocal, exciting, and very entertaining process without which this book would not have been written in this way or within this time frame – or perhaps not at all. Thanks, to Ros Draper, our English editor. Only her kind persistence and ever supportive, thoroughly enjoyable "hands-on" attitude, based on her lifelong and profound professional experience, have made possible the long journey towards the publication of this book in English.

Thanks also to Sidsel Winther, Philip Greve, Anne Christine Petersen, Anders Hagedorn Christensen, Lone Mørch Schneider, Mette-Marie Davidsen, Per Bech Thomsen, and Ulla and Flemming Andersen for making your stories and experiences available to us as inspirational examples in conveying the Dialogue of Acknowledgement. All the examples in the book are authentic. They have either been shared with us or they are transcripts of recordings made during our courses.

Our gratitude goes to Ida Musti Schröder, Claus Neperus, Pernille Hytte Bisgaard, and Ulla Andersen, who have been the constant, tireless, and persistent force behind the Relationship Therapy Centre in terms of researching and developing empirical methods and theory, as well as being responsible for much fun. May we continue in the same vein, undeterred by mammoth agendas. Thanks are also due to Ulla Jørgensen and Linda Jørgensen, without whom the Centre would collapse like a house of cards in a chaotic heap of dust, figures, and documents, with nothing for us to eat or drink.

We are grateful to Ina Elisabeth Munck, who, with great generosity, has shared the entire artistic legacy of the artist Victor IV, pages from his diary, etc., with us and our readers. In a wonderful way, his work has become the book's aesthetic and graphic soul.

We also thank the Imago people. Without your inspiration and provocative inputs we would probably not have been able to gather our experiences and thoughts into this book. We would like to take this opportunity to offer our special thanks to Jette Simon, who first inspired us to do relationship therapy by introducing Imago into Denmark, and who, together with Rick Brown, Maya Kollmann, and the two of us, founded the Danish Imago Institute. Also, thanks to IRI (Imago Relationships International) for space to think, and challenges as well as productive discussions.

We express our appreciation to Hedy and Yumi Schleifer for their professional support, as well as their constant open, brave, vulnerable, and curious search.

Thank you to Ulla and Flemming Andersen, the other couple in our four-leaf clover mini-college, where dialogue and acknowledgement have become cornerstones in our annual month of mutual professional absorption and concentration in a place far from the humdrum of everyday life.

Our thanks to everyone who has read the text closely, critiqued, commented, made suggestions, acknowledged, and given support during the process (in alphabetical order): Ulla and Flemming Andersen, Susanne Bang, Mathias Seidenfaden Busck,

Tina Seidenfaden Busck, Galina Draiby, Søren Bjerrum, Vibeke Hejgaard, Bente Lynge, Anne Mogensen, Birgitte Mønsted, Charlotte Norby, Monette Rostock, Mai-Britt and Martin Schwab, and Susanne Søborg Christensen.

And finally, thank you to all the people – students, customers, clients, weekend couples, and others – who have dared to set out on a journey with one or both of us to explore your relationships with curiosity, daring, desperation, joy, and meaningful interaction. Without our lifelong co-operation with all of you, through thick and thin, this book would not have been written!